God's
home
page

mike riddell

Text copyright © Mike Riddell 1998

The author asserts the moral right
to be identified as the author of this work

Published by
The Bible Reading Fellowship
Peter's Way, Sandy Lane West
Oxford OX4 5HG
ISBN 1 84101 013 8

First published 1998
10 9 8 7 6 5 4 3 2 1 0

Acknowledgments
Unless otherwise stated, Bible quotations are taken from the *New
Revised Standard Version* of the Bible, copyright © 1989 by the
Division of Christian Education of the National Council of the
Churches of Christ in the USA.

Scripture quotations from *The Message* copyright © 1995, 1994,
1995. Used by permission of NavPress Publishing Group.

Extract from 'Knock, knock' by Martin Wroe used by permission.

A catalogue record for this book is available
from the British Library

Printed and bound in Great Britain by
Caledonian International Book Manufacturing Ltd, Glasgow

God's home page

Other books by Mike Riddell

The Insatiable Moon, Flamingo

Godzone, Lion Publishing

alt.spirit@metro.m3, Lion Publishing

Threshold of the Future, SPCK

[CONTENTS]

For Kat

Godspeed on the truest journey...

The Prozac of Preachers

I remember picking up a Gideon's Bible in a seedy Salvation Army hotel in Sydney. The building was called the People's Palace, which is about as big a euphemism as it is possible to use this side of lying. The nicotine-yellow walls complemented the persistent stale aroma of the corridors. Most of the residents were a good deal older and drunker than I was.

I was in one of those emotionally low periods that muddy the transition between youth and adulthood. My druggie/hippie pilgrimage had an element of spiritual search to it. I had experimented with the usual mix of Eastern religious practices, from meditation to astral travelling. An unfortunate sequence of events had left me depressed and lonely in the People's Palace. So it was that I picked up the bedside copy of the Christian scriptures in an act of desperation. I hoped there might be something there for me.

It was a book like any other, it seemed to me, with a table of contents. The New Testament sounded more my cup of tea than the Old Testament, so I turned to the start of that section and began reading. I'm not sure what I expected. Certainly not the extended list of begatting which stretched before me. It was about as exciting as reading the atomic table. In the space of a few minutes, I begat boredom, and tossed the Bible aside.

This encounter with scripture was an unfortunate beginning, but one I am sure that many bemused seekers have shared. That air of mustiness, irrelevance and boredom has attached itself to 'The Bible' like nicotine to smokers. It is history, a tired old tome reeking of antiquity and empire. It has a sort of haunting familiarity to older people, after the fashion of school songs endured at sweaty assemblies. But there is little in the way of interest, vigour, stimulation or challenge. So much is common wisdom.

On the personal front, things changed for me. I eventually became entranced by Jesus of Nazareth, and in my plodding way fell into step behind him. The very scripture that had been closed to me was transformed into my source of life. I began to hunger and thirst for it. Time and again it clubbed me senseless and performed surgery on my soul. It lifted me on wings of discovery, from which I could see vistas to die for. I found myself dazed and bleeding in the presence of the Living God. It were as though after years of disappointment with my television set, someone had shown me that it needed to be plugged in.

No contrast could be greater. I think of my disappointed tossing aside of that Bible in a Sydney hotel room with deep regret. In ignorance, I had neglected a treasure so close at hand. Sadly, as it now seems to me, this casual rejection of scripture has become almost universal. The Bible is neglected by the culture which once romanced it. In contemporary society, it lingers in drawers and on bookshelves with all the raciness of last year's telephone directory.

Sadder still is the fate of the Bible as employed by Christians. In the hands of scholars and preachers, it has become a better tranquillizer than Prozac. I have watched the Pavlovian glazing of eyes in many a church when scripture is read or expounded. For good reason. Years of conditioning have assured the faithful flock that they are about to be relentlessly bored. They can expect to be berated, baffled, instructed, lectured, verbally cudgelled and confounded. As aversion therapy, it is very effective.

The abuse of the Bible is continued by so-called evangelists. Here raw texts are shouted into the wind by men with red faces, who appear angry and vindictive. Pedestrians hurry past to avoid being stung by the lash of a ringing King James verse. Scripture seems to be regarded by such proclaimers of the faith as a magical incantation, capable of stopping people in their tracks and producing instant insight into the meaning of life. Strangely enough, this theory is not supported by evidence.

Perhaps in response to all this, some Christians are starting to turn off the Bible. I seem to encounter increasing numbers of relatively faithful followers of Jesus who have stopped reading scripture. It is not because they are backsliding, reprobate or even opposed to scripture. But the vital connection is missing. It no longer appears to communicate with the complexities of life which they experience on a daily basis. The Bible has ceased to speak for them.

Many such pilgrims have come from solid Evangelical backgrounds, where scripture has occupied an exalted position. They have grown up nurtured on the necessity of daily personal study of the text. Scripture remains subliminally resident in their religious subconscious as the Word of God. They have previously looked to preachers to offer guidance; to expound the scriptures. The net effect of all this is that at the same time as they neglect to read scripture or listen to sermons, they feel guilty about their lapse. Sometimes they will begin programmes or buy books to get them started again. You can find the evidence of this tucked away on bookshelves; a sort of cemetery of good intentions.

To tell the truth, I have felt the pull of these strong currents myself. I find myself at times steering through a fog of indifference, searching for that Promised Land of clarity. I recognize that in certain aspects of my journey with the Bible, I have lost my way. In a sense this book is intended as a self-serving beacon to draw me toward the harbour. My hope is that if it succeeds in that purpose for me, others might find a little light shed on their voyages as well.

But before we seek solutions, we need to be well aware of what the problems are. It could of course be the case that this nascent retreat from scripture is simply a symptom of spiritual laziness. Perhaps a softer generation of Christians has become complacent and drifted from the necessary disciplines of their faith. While this is a possibility to be considered, I suspect that the widespread struggling of thousands of people should not be so lightly dismissed. Forces are at work which are damaging Christian appreciation of scripture, and which require understanding if they are to be addressed.

The emerging culture

It is now almost trite to announce that we live in an age between cultures. But familiarity with the situation does not reduce the significance or the discomfort of occupying such a position. Postmodern times are upon us, which is to say that the old age (modernity) is dying, and the new one (postmodernity) is not wholly apparent as yet. It is one of those transitional times like adolescence, when everything is uncertain and identity is threatened as a consequence. Many values, methodologies and even perceptions are changing around us.

Some aspects of the emerging culture are beginning to take shape. We can already begin to identify a culture which values relationship, immediacy, the interplay of seemingly contradictory codes, a wide tolerance of different belief systems, the ability to function on several levels at the same time, an appreciation of the interconnection of all things and a pick-and-mix approach to faith. Two of the significant trends for the viability of the Bible are post-textuality and the end of metanarratives. It is worth considering each of these in turn, albeit briefly.

The first code-word, post-textuality, we can understand in a greatly simplified fashion by recognizing that the role of literature is diminishing in the new world. People don't read books any more; or to be more truthful, not so many people read not so many books any more. At one time in the not too distant past, books were probably the primary source of information for the majority of the population. Now the written word competes with computers (and related sources), films, music, television and radio. The number of potential inputs is increasing rather than decreasing.

Books suffer (generally) from being linear and progressive. We start at the beginning and follow page by page to the end. This method of assimilating knowledge is comparatively tame in comparison to the possibilities of hypertext (the click-and-travel system of internet navigation) or film subplots, which can lead the participant off in a variety of directions. The written word engages the mind primarily, even though it may evoke other emotions. It does not have the power or excitement of the huge image or the high decibel chord. The limits of text become apparent when compared with other media. The Bible shares the difficulties of other books in this new era.

Regarding the second term, metanarratives, we come close to the heart of the postmodern movement. A metanarrative is a grand story which legitimates a particular worldview by suggesting it is universal. Some commentators have suggested that disbelief in metanarratives is a defining characteristic of postmodernism. Claims to truth which are underwritten by appeal to grand stories are generally regarded as covert attempts to retain or gain power.

In terms of the emerging culture, the Bible is regarded as the mother of all metanarratives. It has served as the legitimating story for the entire Western culture, devastatingly obvious in Christendom. It is not difficult to review history and demonstrate the way in which the Christian metanarrative has gone hand in hand with the pursuit of power. The crusades and the tyranny of certain popes in the Middle Ages bear testimony to the potential for religious abuse. If liberation comes with the discarding of metanarratives, then the Bible has to go.

It has to be admitted that most people wouldn't know a meta-narrative from a milkshake. And yet there is a general unease about claims to scriptural authority. While the shift in culture is not widely reflected upon in philosophic terms, it is experienced at gut level. The resistance to unsubstantiated moral authority is widespread in the Western world, and has implications for how the Bible is received.

Preaching

For many Christians in a busy world, the major interaction they have with the Bible is through preaching. Increasingly negative attitudes to scripture are directly related to the quality of preaching which is demonstrated in churches. Personally I am appalled by the sermons I hear in many congregations. They make me feel sick to the stomach, so that I long for the final blessing to gain some relief. It is only the vestiges of politeness which prevent me from rising to my feet and shouting in frustration that the movement of Jesus Christ should be reduced to this. That and an induced trance-like state of inactivity, akin to that produced by opium.

What is it about such preaching that is so offensive? My first objection is that it is largely cerebral. It engages only the minds of the hearers. Such preaching represents an intellectualizing of the gospel which totally distorts it. The costly practice of following Jesus is reduced to verbal assent to a set of rational propositions. One could be forgiven for assuming that Christianity was a philosophy or set of ideas. A particular problem for the Evangelical tradition, preaching of this variety renders scripture into homogenized pap, from which is extracted a set of 'scriptural principles'. The only response which is then required is agreement with these divine precepts.

Secondly, preaching is often deductive in its methodology; that is, it proceeds from a set of general premises (the text) which are then expounded. The greatest offender in this regard is that school of preaching known as 'expositional'. This is the type of preaching which lingers for six months on a few chapters of Romans. While growing from the finest of motives, that of respect for the text, this approach succeeds often in blunting the impact of the very scripture it seeks to commend. It insists on starting with the text, and uncovering its original meaning before applying it to the present world.

While this sounds like reverence for the Bible, it begins where people are not and often leaves them struggling in the arid wastes of a history they cannot quite imagine. By the time the 'application' is made, the hearers are lost in a world of private reverie. The deductive approach is demonstrably different to the teaching strategy of Jesus, who preferred to start where the people are. His preaching was engaging to the point of provoking people to do him violence. In some settings today the hearers would welcome a little violence, if only to break the tedium.

The authoritarian nature of preaching grows increasingly anachronistic. I remember a billboard I saw outside a church building, which declared 'Church is good for you'. My immediate internal response was 'So's boiled cabbage'. It brought back all the associations of parental authority, of dos and don'ts, of naughtiness and scoldings. Something of this atmosphere remains in some sermons. Whatever is intended, the preaching comes across as a telling-off by an authority figure. The communication is one way and there is no right of reply.

Again the motivation is admirable: it springs from respect for the Word of God. The intent is that we should recognize and 'sit under' the authority of the text. Reformation churches sought to illustrate this architecturally by the elevation of the pulpit to heights which induce vertigo. But this invoking of external authority is positively pre-modern, and liable to rouse resistance amongst people who have grown into and value adulthood. Not even Christian people want to be lectured at by headmasters, and many of them have shown their reaction by ceasing to attend church.

Finally, and most cruelly, much preaching is quite simply boring. In a time when attention spans are plummeting and the means of winning them growing in sophistication, sermons are abysmally dull. I find myself exerting enormous amounts of mental energy during sermons, simply concentrating on the stream of words, out of good-will towards the preacher—wanting this person, against all odds, to inspire me. The effort frequently leaves me with a headache, so at least I have something to take away with me. It is a perfectly natural assumption that at least part of the cause of such ennui is the subject matter: the Bible. Nothing could be further from the truth.

The historical-critical method

The greatest single factor undermining appreciation of scripture is undoubtedly the historical–critical method of textual study. Although it is diminishing in influence rapidly, a whole generation of church leaders and preachers has been schooled in it. Even if they could not describe the technique, they employ it as if it had been passed down from heaven. For many years graduates of theological halls emerged entranced with the discipline of careful exegesis, and applying it with great scrupulosity.

In simple terms, the historical–critical approach to scripture claims that the first step in accurate interpretation of the Bible is to under-stand the origins of a text, and its significance for the original hearers. Only when one has uncovered this primary orientation of scripture may one begin to wrestle with its meaning for today. In consequence, massive resources of biblical scholarship have been directed toward determining the initial and primary meaning of particular texts. Because there are no extant memories of the origins, the process calls for a combination of historical detective work and vigorous specula-tion.

The results are manifold. One is the production of biblical com-mentaries by the acre, all meticulously researched, and most arriving at quite different conclusions than their rivals. A second is an obsess-ion with something which may never be fully known—the original meaning of the text. Postmodernists have recognized the folly of this quest. We simply do not have access to the intended nuances of the author, even in contemporary texts. And certainly any attempt to reach back across thousands of years for assurance will only end in the subtle importing of our own meanings.

But the most damaging of all is the tendency to come at scripture with the mind and analytical tools in hand, as if it were a specimen on the laboratory table to be dissected. Such an approach is thoroughly modernist, and represents the application of the scientific method in fields where it begins to falter. There is something profoundly sad in the attempt to 'prove' the Bible by submitting it to rigorous semantic analysis.

In the hands of preachers (many of whom aspire to be theologians like their teachers), the historical–critical method creates a fixation with introducing their congregations to the basics of ancient Near Eastern anthropology. Great care is taken in making sure that the faithful understand the military practices of the Assyrian Empire. The topography of Palestine and its climatic conditions are expounded with an air of apparent fascination. With not a little pride and delight, our newly ordained expositors explain the intricacies of the aorist tense in the Greek language.

They are often disappointed with their congregation's response. The preacher is excited, inspired and evangelical about the results of the week's preparation of the sermon. He or she strives mightily to light a similar fire in the assembled listeners, but to no avail. Apart from a few intellectuals who enjoy such an approach, the majority stifle yawns and suffer an eye-glazing, skin-crawling, brain-crumbling boredom. They have made the mistake of looking for bread, and instead break their teeth on stones.

Of course all of this is something of a caricature. There have been positive benefits of the application of the historical–critical method. It has helped to reveal covert manipulation of the text by unscrupulous interpreters. And there is real benefit in being able to distinguish the obvious cultural conditioning of the Bible. Slaves and women are but two of the groups who may be grateful for such distinction. But in looking at the marginal position of both preaching and scripture within Western society, the extreme modernism which this approach represents is woefully inadequate. I would be so bold as to argue that we must renounce this way of coming at scripture if it is to come to life for us again.

Armchair faith

Before we laity become too complacent, and content to allocate blame for most things to the clergy, it may be worth reflecting on some problems a little closer to home. One of the causes of dissatisfaction with the Bible might relate to our unwillingness to consider what it has to say. I have discovered that a travel guide is of most use when I plan to take or am engaged on a journey to which the guide relates. While it is possible to read it in isolation, the book will always lack depth and relevance. Perhaps some of our difficulties with scripture stem from a similar tendency to stay at home.

I vividly remember the diminutive but passionate Christian speaker, C.B. Samuel, addressing a gathering of Westerners with aspirations to social change. His life and involvement in villages on the Indian subcontinent left him stunned by the materialistic lifestyle of the West. 'It is not enough,' he puzzled, 'that you sit in your armchair to watch television. It is not enough that you have electricity connected directly to your house, and that the water for your tea runs fresh and clear from a tap. It is not enough that you pull a lever on your chair and a footrest emerges to make you more comfortable. No, you find that you are unable even to rise from your chair to make a selection of channels. You have a remote control so that you can simply point and push a button! And you wonder why you can't understand the Bible!'

The point was well made. There are certain sections of scripture which only make sense when you have responded to earlier challenges. Whatever else it may be, the Bible is a resource book for those who are on a pilgrimage following on the heels of Jesus. It was never intended as an armchair guide for spectators. When we cease to follow, misunderstanding or distortion of scripture soon ensues. If you want to understand the talk, you have to walk the walk. It may well have been Jesus who told a story about a man building a house on sand, and suggested that it had something to do with people who heard but did not act on what they heard.

The culture of busyness

Busyness has become a matter of status in our world. There are a few people who are genuinely busy, and many more who arrange their lives to give the impression of busyness. Who can blame them? It is considered to be a sign of great indolence if a person admits to having spare time. Efficiency is the spirit of the age, and activity is regarded as a sign of productive output. It is a badge of esteem to have people pestering you for your attention—to have messages on the ansaphone, to have a diary full of appointments, to talk on a cellphone while walking or driving. Personally I am not convinced that our lives have any more demands on them than did those of many of our forebears.

However, we have adopted a culture of busyness, so that whether we are busy or not, we certainly feel busy. We tend to rush from project to project, generating a certain breathlessness and urgency. Our lives are filled with 'noise', both literal and figurative. It is extremely difficult for many urban dwellers to be either still or silent. The resultant gap expands like a crevasse under the feet, and participants feel desperately uneasy about it. And so there is a lack of 'space' in our lives; clearings where we might stop and reflect. Everything crowds in upon us, and if we are honest, many of us have come to like it that way. Silence can be dangerous.

The Bible does not take kindly to being jammed into filofax crevices. It is not readily accessible through the technique of scanning for headlines which we employ on the daily newspaper. Scripture is both like and unlike other texts. Its difference from them is evident in how different modes of access will produce markedly different results. I don't believe that encounter with the Bible requires a great deal in terms of quantity of time, but certainly it demands quality of time. Like any book or person who has something to say, it calls for a certain amount of attention in listening. Part of the current neglect of scripture may relate to lives which have no place for it.

Misapprehension

I suspect the Bible has suffered because of the advent of the printing press. Certainly this early technological breakthrough has made scripture available to the masses in ways in which it wasn't previously. However, I think the jury may still be out on whether the gains outweigh the losses. Prior to the printing press, the Bible was generally only available (in laboriously produced manuscripts) to the clergy who were literate and trained in its use, or else was read and preached upon in the communal gathering of the congregation. Now, as it is often touted, the Bible is a bestseller, a book among books.

Except that to approach the Bible as a book is to misapprehend it. It may exist between covers; it may contain sheets of paper with words printed upon them; it may have pages which are numbered sequentially. But here the similarities end. Part of the difficulty of the

Bible is that it looks like a book. Whether we are aware of it or not, we are schooled in ways of relating to books. It is natural, then, that we bring our skills to the collection of scripture. We expect, perhaps, some sort of development. A beginning, an unfolding, an end. We anticipate some sort of consistency of voice, so that a particular theme is unfolded. Because of the expectations we bring, it is easy to end up disappointed.

All of which rather begs the question: if the Bible is not a book, then what is it? That is the task of discovery which will concern the next chapter. For the meantime it is sufficient to say that you need to understand the nature of a beast before attempting to milk it. Otherwise the results may be different from those anticipated!

So, the reasons that many people struggle to connect with the Bible are complex and varied. Some are expressions of the age we live in; some are the legacy of other times. The difficulties are real and serious. But they are insignificant enough in the light of what will be lost if they are not addressed and overcome. Scripture has no more lost its power and majesty than a mountain diminishes simply because it becomes obscured by clouds. Hopefully by the end of this book, the sky may have cleared a little.

1

www.God

In determining what something is, it can be helpful to point out what it is not. This is particularly so when referring to the Bible, which has been around long enough to have something of a history, as they say. Part of the reason people struggle with scripture may be that they are mistaken as to what it is. You can study a train timetable for all you're worth, but it won't reveal much if what you're after is the theory of relativity.

Few documents are as subject to misunderstanding, misuse and abuse as is the Bible. The jolly thing is just so available, and able to be picked up by any nutter with an axe to grind or a silly notion to justify. Every second mass-murderer seems to find it necessary to quote some obscure section of scripture before laying waste the innocent. Televangelists hold it high in their right hand, which does have the effect of drawing attention away from the other hand, which is just as likely in the till.

Let us therefore clear the ground a little by dismissing some of the false accusations as to our defendant's identity.

A book of answers

I have seen answer books, and the Bible is definitely not one. When you look up an answer book, the only bit you are interested in is the little section which gives the correct answer to your question. Some publishers of the Bible have tried to turn it into such a resource by providing a list of situations at the front, and then offering places you can turn to if that is your concern. You may have seen them. 'Masturbation,' they will say, 'see Genesis 38:1–11'. The puzzled self-abuser discovers a totally irrelevant story about Onan which suggests that God killed him for failing to impregnate his sister-in-law. Such information is not immediately helpful.

It is false advertising to suggest that the Bible contains answers to life's questions. Perhaps it is even misleading to imagine that life has answers, in the ordinary understanding of the term. There is a very good Larson cartoon of St Peter outside the Pearly Gates, presenting the aspiring entrants with problems of the kind which start: 'If two vehicles are travelling in opposite directions…' Clearly this is not what life is about, not what God is about, and most certainly not what the Bible is about. Life is not a seventy-year examination to be sat; it is an adventure to be lived.

A book of spells

The Bible is not magic. There we are; I've said it. In and of itself it has no supernatural powers, and is useful for neither curing indigestion nor warding off economic rationalists. The words are very fine in places, I have to admit, and the poetry is majestic. But there are no incantations, spells or secret passwords contained therein. As far as I know, scripture does not restore lost hair or lengthen life in any obvious fashion. People do not become transformed simply by touching a Bible or hearing one quoted in the street.

It would not be necessary to point this out were it not for the ways in which some people use it. A large number of Christians do seem to be under the impression that the Bible contains magic. They memorize sections of it, and then quote it at unbelievers, all the while standing back and waiting for the miraculous conversion which is about to happen. It is the Christian equivalent of alchemy, and about as successful in achieving its end. If there are spells in the Bible, they are usually of fine weather and called droughts.

A divine verbatim

Muslims consider that the Qur'an was dictated to the Prophet by Allah, and therefore contains the direct speech of God. The Bible makes no such grandiose claims. News that the Christian scriptures are not regarded as verbatim quotes from God will come as a great relief to people who would otherwise be under the impression that the Deity is excessively verbose and showing definite signs of repetitive confusion. It would be hard to take seriously anyone who compared breasts to gazelles.

There are of course bits which claim to be prophetic in that they represent the voice of God speaking through someone, but for the most part the Bible does not claim to be dictated by God, and we could imagine there are sections which are frankly embarrassing to the Trinity. The bashing of babies' skulls against rocks (Psalm 137:9) may be an understandable expression of anger against our enemies, but is hardly an indication of divine love. And while Paul might have found long hair on a man not to his taste (1 Corinthians 11:14), it is probably a bit strong to universalize his predilection as a dictum of existence.

It is a lot easier to relax in the divine presence once you realize that you don't have to swallow the scriptures whole as a facsimile transmission from the heavenly throne. To speak of the Bible as 'the Word of God' is at best an analogy and at worst misleading. God does indeed speak, but to the best of our knowledge has yet to record memoirs.

A handbook of doctrine

I'm afraid I need to disappoint even the Calvinists. The Bible is not a theological textbook. It contains no systematic theology at all, though it does have some rather unsystematic and positively disorderly theology. Scholars of the church have been wont to regard scripture as a compendium of doctrine. They produce truckloads of books demonstrating exactly which doctrines the Bible upholds, and giving numerous scriptural references to substantiate their claims. I'm convinced that nobody ever looks the references up, because it gets in the way of following the argument.

Doctrine is a poor substitute for scripture. It is like cans of homogenized babyfood, which have exotic labels such as 'chicken and vegetables' or 'pork and rice', but which usually contain identical pap. Doctrines often turn out to be mechanisms by which one group of people can lay hold on the truth and exert power over those 'in error'. The Bible, on the other hand, is very subversive. It is considered far too unruly to be distributed in its raw state; hence the need to put it through the doctrinal blender to make it digestible.

An instruction manual

I used to covet publications which went by the title of 'workshop manuals'. Each one was devoted to a particular model of car, and contained all the technical details which one needed to effect repairs. They illustrated such mechanical wonders as 'worm-drive spigots', and revealed how to install a new one. Attractive as such manuals are, the Bible is not one of them. It neither contains diagrams of the inner workings of the human heart nor gives procedures for psychoanalysis.

I have heard Christians say of scripture, 'When all else fails, try reading the manual'. Generally, however, the Bible does not respond to this sort of treatment. If you have a malignant tumour and are trying to decide whether to undergo chemotherapy, it will take some time thumbing through the pages of scripture before help is obtained. People are not machines, and God is not a mechanic. The spiritual life, in many instances, is not about fixing things at all, but about knowing how to live in an unfixed state. This requires more than a manual.

A collection of moral precepts

Morality has a high profile these days, especially in certain religious circles. Such morality usually has to do with something akin to the social conventions of the middle class, rather than issues of justice and mercy. A large number of the proponents of the moral life assume that they are expressing the essence of the Bible, and claim it as their foundation at the same time as calling others to live by it. However, neither God nor the Bible stack up very well under the intense moral scrutiny common to such moralogians. Scripture at various junctures encourages lying, winks at murder, allows prostitution and forgives adultery.

The book of Proverbs does offer some comfort to those with a puritanical bent. But as many scholars have noted, the very same section of scripture sticks out as a bit of a sore thumb in relation to the rest of the material to be found there. The Jewish Law as found in the Pentateuch provides a little hope for death-by-stoning advocates and other religious sadists, but the hope is short-lived as the Gospels stand the Law on its head. All in all, those looking in the Bible for a systematic moral code will be searching in vain.

Despite the fact that someone has recently made the attempt to rewrite it as one, the Bible is not a novel. It is not one story; it doesn't progress in any linear fashion; and there is no clear plot. Narrative is a big part of it, and there are some fine short stories contained within it. But scripture was never intended to be read like a book, and usually disappoints those who come to it with that intention. There are of course many great characters—too many to be able to gain an overview of their interrelationship. In the end, you have to accept that the Bible is not 'a good read', in the sense of books to take away on holiday.

None of this is intended to be detrimental to scripture, or to diminish respect for it. The purpose is to rid ourselves of distorted images of the Bible, which tend to blind us to much more than they reveal. The dignity of scripture is such that it does not need false representations for the purposes of marketing. It is well able to stand on its own feet. It is time now to give some thought as to what the real nature of the Bible is.

God's home page

So what's the Bible about? Is there anything it may be compared to in order to get a handle on it? I think there is. As long as we don't push the analogy too far, I believe we might reasonably compare the Bible to a website associated with the living God: God's home page. It may be worth looking at some elements of this comparison to see what implication it has for our relationship with scripture.

A site for sore eyes

Apart from the recorded experiences of some mystics and prophets, there sometimes seems to be little hope of direct connection with God for most of us. Stumbling pilgrims like ourselves who collect lint between our toes and lose our dry-cleaning tickets will probably not experience a direct theophany between home and the chip shop. For whatever reason, God doesn't lurk about the place in blindingly obvious fashion. The whole performance is a great deal more subtle than that.

But God has not left the universe vacant. For those who are interested, there are pointers all over the show. Ambiguous, fragmentary pointers; but definite hints, none the less. Perhaps you've come across them in the so-called 'natural order', or in people who have been special. I suspect that the Bible represents a pointer to divine loitering more tangible and accurate than most. It is not, as I have been at pains to establish, a direct connection with God. But neither does a website link one immediately with its creator. It is an intermediate place, a location somewhere between the cybersurfer and the hyperauthor, where the two can meet and interact.

When someone produces a home page, it's because they want to be present out there in cyberspace. Not physically present, but available in a representational sense. If someone were to do a search for a particular person, they might come across a site which would give them some clues as to that person's identity and character. It's this sort of connection which the Bible offers to humanity on behalf of God. The initiative, as with any home page, lies with its Creator. But response and further interaction are in the hands of the visitor.

The Bible is a site which is out there for those who are looking. Somewhere beyond it lies God. Visitors can have a bit of a scout about in it. They can sit down with a cup of coffee in hand and explore the links. Unless they particularly want it, there will be no direct link to God Almighty. But it's a site which rewards a little poking around in, especially for those who might be travel-weary or cyber-sated.

Interesting bits

When you're setting up a home page, you have to think about what you're going to put on it. It has to convey something of the complexity of your personality to the outside world; it's a shopfront for the psyche. The whole exercise can become one of integration. It involves the pulling together of all sorts of diverse stuff which only coheres because of its relationship with the author. When it comes to construction of the site, you often end up dredging your hard drive and collecting what a good friend of mine calls 'bits'. These may have accumulated over years, and represent a whole range of previous contexts and personae. But you bung them in there to fill up space and flesh out the picture.

The Bible is like that. It is a collection of bits. The bits don't always fit together very well—sometimes they even seem to be contradictory. Stories, poems, teachings, records, events and miracles rub up against each other. They come from all over the place, and span at least 4,000 years of history. What holds all these bits together is the fact that they somehow represent the continued involvement of God with the world in general and humanity in particular. God's system memory is bigger than most, and so there's a lot of stuff that's been assembled for the site. Basically, the Bible is a gathering of God's bits.

In a previous era, we might have talked about scripture as God's shoebox. Having my origins in that distant time when a hard disk was probably a cough lozenge, I still have a shoebox. It contains scraps of paper which have been significant enough to stash away and keep. Frankly, to read some of it now makes me blush. But I keep it because it is a part of my journey; integral to the person I now am. I wouldn't mind giving people access to the shoebox, provided they didn't hold me to account for everything they found there. They would need to understand it for what it was: a collection of my interesting bits.

In the same way, the Bible contains fragments relating to God's dealings with humanity over a long period of time. It is possible to rummage through them, and to think about what they reveal about both God and humanity. To come back to the analogy of a home page, scripture gives a feel for the style and interests of God, rather than being a direct communication from God. It would be a mistake to read too much into it. Take this delightful verse from 1 Kings 14:10, in the King James Version:

> *Therefore, behold, I will bring evil upon the house of*
> *Jeroboam, and will cut off from Jeroboam him that pisseth*
> *against the wall, and him that is shut up and left in Israel,*
> *and will take away the remnant of the house of Jeroboam, as*
> *a man taketh away dung, till it be all gone.*

To read this in isolation would be completely mystifying. It doesn't make any sense because it is simply a fragment which has come from a distant era and culture. Fortunately, with a little hypertext exploration, the context emerges and male readers can relax again in the urinal. It's just a bit of stuff from the divine archives.

Navigating the site

Thinking back to my experience in the People's Palace of Sydney, my problem was that I entered God's home page by the back door. Like many others before me, I stumbled across a section of genealogy which failed to engage my deeper passions, and led to my tossing scripture aside. This is the problem with binding the Bible between covers and giving it the appearance of being a book. One generally reads a book from start to finish, with a reasonable expectation of a beginning, a middle and an end. Sadly, while the Bible gives every outward impression of being a book, it simply doesn't work like that.

A website is a much better analogy for how the various parts of scripture are connected. There is no linear progression to the truck stops of cyberspace. They have a front page, certainly, and that is the best place to enter the site from. But a 'front page' is not the same as the 'first page' of a book. Thanks to the magic of hypertext, websites contain labyrinthine pathways based on relationship rather than order. A home page allows intuitive and multi-directional roaming through the accumulated material. It neither requires nor rewards a linear approach.

Without pushing the analogy too far, the Bible operates in a similar way. We will look later at what the 'front page' of scripture is. In the meantime, let us be aware that the assembled parts of the Bible are collected in a somewhat haphazard fashion. To push them into chronological order requires a great deal of scholarship, and runs the danger of doing violence to the material. A much more fruitful approach is to 'visit' the various pages of the site, and to be content with browsing rather than organizing.

An interactive environment

Any website worth its salt contains interactive elements. It's not all dished up to you on a plate; there are things you can do which will widen the scope of the experience and perhaps provide more understanding. Questions can be pursued and mysteries followed. The Bible is very much like this. It responds well to prodding and poking; to exploring its outer territory and inner meaning. Because of its interactivity, scripture provides a multi-level experience. What you get out of it depends in large part on what you bring to it. The same site can engage children and yet satisfy the most complex longings of sophisticated searchers after truth.

The secret of the Bible is that it is a living site. To cynics and rationalists it gives the appearance of a dead text, having an interest for the history of religion, but little else. They can study it, analyse it, chop it up into pieces and determine its genetic origins—and yet fail to engage with it at all. They are like forensic experts who cut up a musical score and report on the shape and colour of the various notes, without ever having heard the music played. The Bible is a shy context. It only opens up to those who bring their heartfelt questions to it, and are prepared to spend a little time searching.

The wonder of an interactive site is that it expands before your eyes. The further you delve into it, the more of its mysteries it gives up to you. Long-time explorers begin to pick up valuable knowledge of the main features of the site, but the further out they get, the more it continues to develop in response. The Bible has proved adequate to whole lifetimes of exploration. Just when you think you've got it sussed, it takes you off into some previously untravelled territory. As an old hymn about scripture has it, 'The Lord has yet more light and truth to break forth from his word'. There is no end to God's home page. It is capable of keeping participants up well into the night.

Getting on line

There is an old story of the priest who was resident in a very poor parish. The church building was falling down, sparrows were nesting in the sanctuary and the roof leaked in the rain. Many members of the congregation struggled to put food on the table of an evening. In desperation, the priest prostrated himself before the altar and cried out to God: 'Please, Lord, won't you let me win the lottery? I promise before you that I'll only spend the money on your house and your people.' Saturday came and went, and the priest didn't get any prizes at all. He took his case to God: 'Look at the state of this building,' he said. 'What sort of impression does this give people of you? I plead with you, Lord, grant me first prize in the lottery!'

This time he was sure the message had got through. He waited with excitement for the results to be announced. But once again he had won not a sausage. By this stage the priest was getting angry. He marched up to the altar and harangued God. 'It's no wonder you can't get anyone to follow you,' he chided, 'if this is the way you treat your people. Here I am, your faithful servant, trying to do your work, and you won't even answer my simple prayer to win the lottery. Look at me, have mercy on your people; grant us first prize.' With that there was a flash of light, a trumpet sounded, and a voice boomed out from behind the altar: 'All right,' it said, 'I hear you. I'll tell you what: how about you meet me halfway and buy a ticket?'

It would be fruitless to attempt to browse the web without first securing an internet connection. You could sit behind your computer and abuse it to your heart's content, but without being on line, it is unlikely to take you far. To access God's home page in any meaningful way, it is necessary to have a connection. Fortunately, we come with all the necessary software and hardware. It is bundled with the condition of humanity. But as with all programmes, it has to be set up. The link needs to be made. It is not difficult to do, apart from being the hardest thing in the universe. It requires faith. Faith is the active ingredient in connecting with the divine website.

Openness to the possibility of God and a searching heart represent the system requirements for getting on line. Of course the Bible is accessible to everyone, with or without faith. But the true depths and heights of it require that the interactive features are installed and operating. And this in turn demands the risk of trusting God. Unfortunately, the features of the Bible are not demonstrable to those who are not willing to take the chance. It's all there for the asking, but you still have to buy the ticket. In fact, when it comes to scripture, the ticket is free. But you do need to want it.

After all, the Bible is primarily a resource for those who are interested in connecting with God. It is a working site for those who have decided to follow the divine lure wherever it may lead. Sure, you can look at the site without commitment, and even get some rough idea of what it contains. But it will never come to life or reveal its secrets to those who do not have an account there. To exhaust the analogy totally and leave it wobbling on its last legs, there is even a password to establish an account. It is in the public domain. It consists of a name: 'Jesus Christ'.

So there we have it. God's home page, with all the detritus of the ages attached. Unfortunately present to most of us in the guise of a book, and subject to various kinds of abuse through misunderstanding. In the scope of this reflection on the Bible, we will endeavour to map some of the main features of its cyberian topography, and demonstrate its capabilities. In order to make the most use out of such a guide, you need to establish a connection. Talking about exploration is a second-order activity. It's much more fun to log on and take the thing for a spin yourself.

Dangerous Memory

Without the benefit of memory, identity would be a hard thing to hang on to. You would need to keep reinventing yourself every few seconds. Oliver Sacks in his delightful book *The Man Who Mistook his Wife for a Hat*[1] describes a man who has just such a condition. Jimmie G.'s short-term memory is practically non-existent, so that he cannot even recall events of a few minutes earlier. In his original medical notes, Sacks wrote of Jimmie: 'He is, as it were, isolated in a single moment of being, with a moat or lacuna of forgetting all round him… He is man without a past (or future), stuck in a constantly changing, meaningless moment.'

In many respects, this is not a bad description of Western society today. There seems to be a conspiracy of amnesia which leaves us 'stuck in a constantly changing, meaningless moment'. The seduction of novelty seems to have loosened our hold on heritage. Fortunately, there are many resources to help us connect with our past, and to remind us where the roots of our identity lie. It is a mistake to dwell in the past, but it is equally errant to ignore or misunderstand the past. Family photo albums are both sacramental and therapeutic.

Some amnesia, like that of Jimmie G., is accidental and tragic. But there are also varieties of forgetting which are quite intentional. There is protective forgetting, which is an internal process by which memories too painful for the conscious mind are suppressed. And then there is evasive forgetting. This is the attempt to conceal the past because knowledge of it threatens the present. Such deliberate and manipulative amnesia is generally associated with those who have a stake in keeping the present the way that it is.

When I first came to Christian faith, I did not initially attend gatherings of the institutional church. Instead, a group of dissolute hippies like myself would gather in homes, and read and discuss the Bible. This continued for some two years. I am eternally grateful for the circumstances which meant I came at scripture in separation from the church. It introduced me to the heart of the Christian tradition in relatively unadulterated form. I had instant access to the memory banks of the faith. It has stood me in good stead when encountering those who attempt to suppress the dangerous memory of the living God.

Institutional drift

In order to preserve things over time, institutions are necessary. They are the bodily form and skeletal structure which sustains whatever life they carry. Without them there is no continuity, and it is a pointless exercise to complain of their existence. However, there is a dark side to institutional life. Almost invariably, there is the tendency for institutions to lose sight of the life they exist to preserve, and to become instead ends in themselves. The mechanisms of institutional survival —hierarchy, power, structure, control, indoctrination—are used to foster the institution itself, and to protect those who live within it.

For their own honesty and relevance, institutions need perpetual challenge and renewal; a constant call to remain true to their purpose. Unfortunately, it is just such a call to renewal which institutional structures tend to resist like the devil. When the focus is on preservation, change is perceived as a threat to survival. The sanctions of the institution against reformers are deadly and enduring. The longer the structure exists, the more adept it becomes at managing dissent and stifling opposition. Such behaviour is not necessarily wilful; it is simply the way in which institutions operate.

Religions develop institutional life. Wishing it were otherwise does not change reality. In a historical faith like Christianity, there is an extremely important tradition to be guarded and passed on. Such is the responsibility of the church. And like it or not, the church is an institution. As such it is subject to all the currents of institutional calcification, and a brief survey of church history will more than illustrate the existence of the dark side of institutional life within Christianity. The church suffers from a condition which might be termed ecclesiastical hardening of the arteries.

In fact the history of the people of God is the history of encounter between spirit and form. The living God moves alongside and ahead of the people, guiding them from age to age. And more often than not the religious functionaries—those who are supposed to be the servants of God—become God's enemies through their attempts to regulate what God may or may not get up to. They seek to preserve their positions and maintain their control over the people of God; a desire which is antithetical to God's anarchistic tendencies.

To the great credit of the institutional church, it has continued to carry within it the extremely subversive material of scripture. At the centre, of course, is Jesus. His struggle against and disgust with those who would stifle God from within the religious structures is plainly evident:

> *But woe to you, scribes and Pharisees, hypocrites! For you lock people out of the kingdom of heaven. For you do not go in yourselves, and when others are going in, you stop them.*
> *(Matthew 23:13, 14)*

But Jesus exemplifies a long history of the prophets, rather than being the exception to it, in taking to task the institutional abuses of the religious hierarchy. The Bible resolutely resists the co-option of faith for venal purposes.

The pursuit of power

Leadership easily gets into bed with power. The very process of attaining positions of leadership can be the result of promiscuous encounters with institutional gatekeepers. Power, of course, is supremely seductive and hugely addictive. Those who have it can't get enough of it, and usually want more. That which they have is fiercely protected. Human history is littered with the casualties of power plays. Such is the way of the world and the stuff of politics.

The institutional church clearly needs leaders. It should not be surprising that leadership roles in the church attract similar sorts of Machiavellian manoeuvrings to those outside it. Anyone who has experienced life on the inside of the church will have experienced this dark side of ecclesial life. From the bands of monks who would beat up opponents in early Christological councils, to spiritual and sexual abuse by prominent television preachers, the church's leaders have been far from pristine. The pursuit of power and its trappings is as common as communion amongst the people of God.

But to their embarrassment, status-seeking leaders of the church find themselves presiding over a tradition which undermines their authority. The dangerous memory of God which the Bible preserves threatens to erupt at any time in judgment against them:

> *Thus says the Lord God: Ah, you shepherds of Israel who have been feeding yourselves! Should not shepherds feed the sheep? You eat the fat, you clothe yourselves with the wool, you slaughter the fatlings; but you do not feed the sheep. You have not strengthened the weak, you have not healed the sick, you have not bound up the injured, you have not brought back the strayed, you have not sought the lost, but with force and harshness you have ruled them. (Ezekiel 34:2–4)*

And thanks again to scripture, we know that the very Jesus who is proclaimed by such 'fat shepherds' represents an entirely opposing perspective on the relationship between leadership and power.

> *So Jesus called them and said to them, 'You know that among the Gentiles those whom they recognize as their rulers lord it over them, and their great ones are tyrants over them. But it is not so among you; but whoever wishes to become great among you must be your servant, and whoever wishes to be first among you must be slave of all. (Mark 10:42–44)*

Reformers of the church have found in scripture a place to stand; a viewing platform from which to measure and critique the community of faith. It knocks the stuffing out of pretension and autocracy. There can be few other institutions which would tolerate the existence of such revolutionary teaching, let alone make it available to its adherents.

It has not escaped the attention of many an entrepreneur that there is a quid to be made out of religion. The great masses of people are gratifyingly interested in questions of deep meaning and salvation. If you can simply control access to what it is they are looking for, there is a steady and lucrative market to be exploited. In the early days of the movement, it was the temple which was at the centre of religious life, and the business of sacrifice was the main game. Various sharp agents made a few bob out of providing the necessaries to faithful pilgrims. Until Jesus put the cat among the pigeons, that is.

> *In the temple he found people selling cattle, sheep and doves,*
> *and the money changers seated at their tables. Making a whip*
> *of cords, he drove all of them out of the temple, both the sheep*
> *and the cattle. He also poured out the coins of the money*
> *changers and overturned their tables. He told those who were*
> *selling the doves, 'Take these things out of here! Stop making*
> *my Father's house a marketplace!' (John 2:14–16)*

In the Middle Ages, the bureaucrats of the church stumbled on the idea of selling indulgences. According to the ecclesiastical orthodoxy which they promoted, the spirits of the dear departed could be released from purgatory through the payment of generous donations to the church. My favourite ditty from that era is this: 'As soon as the coin in the coffer rings, the soul from purgatory springs'. Advertising jingles have a long history! Today we do nothing so tacky, apart that is from suggesting that tithing is a form of divine investment with excellent returns, and hawking mass-produced icons and pre-blessed hankies.

The marketing of God is, as I have said, dependent on controlling access. You can't charge people for something which is available else-where free. Hence the notion of the priestly channelling of the divine presence, to keep the unwashed flock fenced off from the big G. In 1536, William Tyndale was burned for the crime of translating the Bible into readable English; the bishops were deeply fearful of what might happen if ordinary people had access to scripture. In defiance of such tyranny, however, the Bible keeps alive the dangerous notion that the mercy of God is freely available.

> *Ho, everyone who thirsts, come to the waters; and you that have no money, come, buy and eat! Come, buy wine and milk without money and without price. (Isaiah 55:1)*

Scripture assures us that the love of God is something which can't be bought and sold, but is available in abundance to any who want it. It's hard to work too many angles on that sort of deal.

Living with a tiger

For the institutional church, then, living with the Bible is the equivalent of cohabitation with a tiger. In the absence of any direct advice on the matter from Calvin (of the American cartoon Calvin & Hobbes, rather than John), I assume there are some practical considerations to adopting such a lifestyle. It might be interesting to compare such pointers on living with a tiger to the way in which scripture is treated by the church.

Keep your distance

Tigers can jump a long way. It pays to keep as far out of reach as possible. Obviously you don't want to be so far away that you can't see it, but neither do you want to be so close that it might bite you in the backside.

Get on friendly terms

There's no point in making an enemy of a tiger, if you can possibly avoid it. Pretend that you really like it by making reassuring noises about how wonderful and important a beast it is. Try not to reveal that you are scared of it.

Pull its teeth and claws

This is very good advice, providing you can get close enough to perform the operation. You may have to employ someone to do it for you. But you will sleep much better once you know the really dangerous parts have been removed.

Try to keep it contained

A loose tiger is a dangerous tiger. The best possible scenario is to keep it under control. It is particularly important not to turn your back on a tiger. Wherever possible make sure it is kept within certain boundaries.

Remind it who's boss

Never let a tiger get the upper hand, or you'll live to regret it. From the earliest opportunity, remind the tiger that you're in charge, and that without your care it would have a very sorry life indeed. It's your tiger, not vice versa.

Don't get it excited

Even when you've got it reasonably under control, a tiger which gets overly excited might attack. Be calm and rational when addressing your tiger. Keep it away from small children who may be tempted to treat it with insufficient care.

Clean up the mess

Unfortunately, given that tigers are extremely hard to house-train, they tend to produce quite a mess in their wake. This should be removed as quickly as possible, before it creates a stink.

A little reflection at this point on the handling of scripture within the institutional church might bring to light a few parallels with the care of tigers. In a largely unconscious desire for control, the ecclesiastical machine has acted to minimize the danger and discomfort of harbouring the Bible. Measures for confinement and mastery are well understood and effectively applied.

Out from under

It is not only the institutional church which has difficulties with the Bible. Petty dictators, tyrannical states, oppressive regimes and military juntas have all felt nervous about the potential of scripture to undermine their authority. It is, after all, a universally available revolutionary manifesto. The Bible suggests a trans-national, trans-historical and trans-political locus of authority; one that is beyond the control of political power. At its heart is an irrepressible call for justice, and a strong affirmation of the accountability of leaders.

Israel's foundational encounter with God came when the Egyptians were sticking it up them through the imposition of slave labour.

In response God appears to Moses and declares:

> *'I have observed the misery of my people who are in Egypt; I have heard their cry on account of their taskmasters. Indeed, I know their sufferings, and I have come down to deliver them from the Egyptians...' (Exodus 3:7, 8)*

The resultant saga of frogs, flies and freedom leaves the Pharaoh in no doubt that the short-term benefits of slavery are outweighed by the consequences.

There is a marked absence of forelock-tugging in scripture. In the well-known story of Shadrach, Meshach and Abednego, Jewish political prisoners of the Babylonian Empire get uppity (Daniel 3). They refuse to bow down to a golden image as demanded by the king, and instead tell him where to put it. By surviving the mini-holocaust which they are subjected to, the rebels assert their independence. And then in the New Testament, we find the apostle Peter making this revolutionary declaration to the powers-that-be in Jerusalem: 'We must obey God rather than any human authority' (Acts 5:29).

This is not dusty historical stuff. In South America, in South Africa, in Poland and the former Soviet Union, people who read the Bible have refused to accept ideological totalitarian rule. In America, it was no coincidence that the leaders of the civil rights movement were preachers. The dangerous memory of scripture has disembowelled the corporate illusion of state propaganda, reminding citizens that they need not be subject to authority which has no respect for justice or people. In reading the Bible, they find a perspective which is free from ideological blinkers, and which inspires them to resist.

One of the most important and revolutionary functions of the Bible is to remind people who they are. Over the droning voices of indoctrination which label human beings as peasants, serfs, beggars, outcasts, foreigners, slaves, inmates, patients, consumers or subjects, scripture asserts that in essence, people are the children of God. There is the ringing affirmation which the apostle Peter writes to a bunch of slaves: 'Once you were not a people, but now you are God's people' (1 Peter 2:10). Paul declares: 'For all who are led by the Spirit of God are children of God' (Romans 8:14). The effect of these words is to provide an unshakeable sense of belonging and inalienable dignity.

Assurance of identity is a powerful force. It may not be too much of a simplification to say that many of the problems that humanity encounters are born of a lapse in memory—we momentarily forget who we are. It is possible to believe the lies which are foisted upon us, and accept limitations which are uncalled for. In order to maintain a resistance against such distortions, we need to remind ourselves again and again of who we are and what we are about. When we know that, we are empowered to live and die out of an inner sense of freedom and security. It is a dangerous and liberating memory.

Waking the West

A story from *Godzone*:[2]

> *In a far-off country there was a small village in the midst of a forest. The village holy man was a person of great spiritual power. When any calamity threatened his people, he would go into a certain part of the forest to meditate. There he would light a fire, say a special prayer, and God would hear him and save the people from disaster. When the time came for him to die, he passed his mantle to a younger sage. He was also wise, but he lacked some of the spiritual power of his master. When trouble threatened, he went to the sacred place in the forest and cried out, 'Merciful God, forgive me! I don't know how to light the fire, but I am still able to say the prayer.'*
> *God heard and the miracle was performed.*

> *In the next generation, this man's disciple would go into the forest and say, 'I don't know how to light the fire, I've forgotten the prayer, but I know the place and I pray this is enough.' It was enough and again salvation was granted. When it fell to the next in the line of village sages to seek God's help, he was distraught. Sitting in his hut, his head in his hands, he spoke in anguish: 'I am unable to light the fire, and I don't know the prayer, and I cannot even find the place in the forest. All I can do is to tell the story, trusting in God. I only hope it is sufficient.' And it was sufficient.*

So far so good. But what happens when even the story is forgotten? Jimmie G. was 'isolated in a single moment of being, with a moat or lacuna of forgetting all round him'. The film *Twelve Monkeys* featured a character with a memory which had been replaced with an alternative, but which continually threatened to re-emerge. It sometimes seems to me as we enter the rapids of postmodernity that the whole of Western culture is suffering from terminal amnesia regarding what human life is all about. A spinning carousel of entertainment, consumption, noise and activity has replaced the agenda of spiritual growth and development.

As the last vestiges of Christendom fade from the culture, it is a frenetic but essentially barren landscape that we are left with. Fascination with monetarist economics seems to have produced societies in which fellow human beings are regarded as competitors for resources rather than members of a shared community. The end of human life has been trivialized into a race to collect possessions. All spaces in existence are occupied, in an apparent fear of silence or free time. We have suffered the commodification of the universe.

Humanity is more than all this. It is not that I want a return to Christendom, when the church held sway over the whole of society, or even that I hope for the conversion of the majority of the population. It is simply that we need to recover something of the story of what it means to be human, if we are to avoid destroying ourselves and the planet with us. In this regard, scripture helps us to recall what some of the basic elements of the story are. God's home page can serve to remind us of such qualities as responsibility, mercy, love, relationship, dependence, humility and stillness. It can restore that which has been lost: the recollection that we are made for a purpose.

Total subversion

Everyone knows the story of Rosa Parks. She wasn't looking to make trouble. She was just tired, and had sore feet. Boarding a bus, she sat down in an empty seat and rested her weary legs. When the bus filled up, and the driver demanded she stand up so that a white man could sit down, she refused. It wasn't that she had any intention of making a statement, or sparking a political campaign. She just had sore feet, and didn't want to stand. The driver threatened to call the police. 'Call them,' she said. And Rosa thought about how you continually put yourself out for white folks, and they don't even treat you like a human being.

It turned out to be the spark which ignited the entire civil rights movement. It was a classic case of a dangerous memory. Orthodoxy in Montgomery was that white people were better than black people, and therefore they had rights and privileges which were denied their African American fellow citizens. But on 1 December, 1955, Rosa Parks remembered that she was a human being, with equal claims to dignity and respect. White America regarded this memory as dangerous, and that judgment proved correct. The nation was plunged into turmoil as competing views of human community clashed.

Where did Rosa Parks' memory come from? On what basis did she feel justified in challenging racial prejudice? Certainly we would want to claim an innate sense of justice for her, and perhaps a little weary bloody-mindedness. But it would be remiss to overlook the fact that Rosa Parks was a church member. Every Sunday, she listened to preaching from the Bible which reminded her that whatever else happened, she was a child of God. She read for herself that there was nothing in heaven or on earth which could separate her from the love of God. Rosa Parks had been corrupted by some very subversive scriptures.

The Bible is by nature subversive. It sows seeds of dissent wherever it is read, by offering an alternative reading of reality, independent of any other authority. It is irrepressible. Through its keeping alive of the dangerous memory of divinely purposed humanity, it has brought down empires, kingdoms, governments and institutions. For all those who would regard it as reactionary and moralistic, there are hordes of witnesses who will testify to the way in which it has freed them from slavery, oppression and prejudice.

By comparing human institutions with the dreaming of God for an integrated future, the Bible relativizes all political programmes. By measuring rulers and powermongers against the compassionate and self-sacrificial nurture of God, the Bible undermines all unjust claims to authority. By evaluating the church against the life-giving, Spirit-filled movement of God in the world, the Bible exposes all religious game-playing. By assessing the human lust for power and wealth against the grace and generosity of God, the Bible inspires the hope of a more meaningful and rewarding approach to life.

The divine website grants access to humanity's family photo album. By browsing through it, we are reminded of where we have come from and to whom we belong. We recognize ourselves and others, and gain a greater sense of our place in the overall scheme of things. It can be a sobering experience, to remember. There are parts which we would rather gloss over, or keep secret. But there they are, confronting us, as we move from page to page. And once you have discovered the dangerous memory of scripture, it continues to haunt. That's the way in which subversion operates; you can never look at the world or yourself in the same way again.

Take Me to your Leader

Atheists take heart. The Bible says there is no God. Not many people know that. But there it is, plain as the nose on your face, in Psalm 14: 'Fools say in their hearts, "There is no God."' Which is by way of demonstrating that you can support any position you like through the judicious quoting of scripture. Not only is this possible, it is also prevalent. Nutters with a religious bent fossick about in the extremities of the Bible, discovering verses like 'Therefore kill every male among the little ones, and kill every woman' (Numbers 31:17) to support their psychotic lifestyles. Politicians discover that by and large, God is on their side. Military juntas find a few select words to use as a byline for their despotic rule.

The Bible is a big collection. You can do pretty much anything with it if you have a mind to. And even more without a mind. It's like using the Encyclopaedia Britannica to justify picking your nose—there's bound to be something there to bolster your position. But scripture was never intended to be a source book for reinforcing ideologies, any more than the Encyclopaedia Britannica exists for the benefit of nose pickers. The Bible is God's home page and, naturally enough, its main subject matter is God. In our encounter with it, we begin to discover who this God person is, and what meaning that could possibly have for our lives.

Because people have treated the Bible as if it were a book, they tend to enter it from funny angles, and so end up with unusual ideas about God. As well as asserting that there is no God, scripture can be used to establish that God is war-mongering, jealous, vengeful, genocidal, racist, egotistical and homophobic. The Bible has also been used to prove what time in the morning the world began, and why the earth is the centre of the universe. Each of these approaches is fundamentally flawed, and demonstrates the programmer's maxim: rubbish in, rubbish out.

To make sense of www.God, you need to enter through the front page. And the front page of God's home page is Jesus of Nazareth. If you treat the Bible as a book, you don't come across Jesus in any recognizable sense until you're three-quarters of the way through. This belies the fact that Jesus is the centre, the heart and the fulcrum of scripture. If you go searching through cyberspace for God, the place you're looking for is the Gospels; the earliest recorded stories about Jesus. That's the front page from which all other scriptural exploration needs to begin.

God's front page

Stories about a man who lived two thousand years ago may seem a strange choice for God to put up front on the website. What is it about Jesus that is so important anyway?

Jesus the Word of God

Words are delightful. They are primarily vehicles of communication. By using them, people are able to connect with each other. Words can carry emotions, ideas, commitments, visions and invitations. If the attempted communication works, something which is in my heart or mind is transported to yours in such a way that it evokes a response. As someone for whom words are my trade, I have great respect for the mystery and power of them.

To say that Jesus is the Word of God is to say that God wants to communicate with humanity, and that Jesus represents the essence of that desire to talk. A person's word is a part of them; when it is offered to another, a part of themselves is offered with it. Jesus, the Word of God, is God's word to us which contains most of what needs to be said. Jesus is the self-communication of God:

*In the beginning was the Word, and the Word was with God,
and the Word was God... And the Word became flesh and
lived among us, and we have seen his glory, the glory as of a
father's only son, full of grace and truth. (John 1:1, 14)*

Some people talk about the Bible as the Word of God. This is a fundamental misunderstanding. God cannot be contained in words on a page, but only accessed through a living person. The Bible contains the Word of God because it gives access to God through Jesus. And it can become the Word of God for us once we have established our own personal account through Jesus. But Jesus is a part of God; in fact we would want to say (as long as you know what is meant) that Jesus is God. Scripture is merely a witness to God.

Jesus the face of God

The trouble with the presence of God in the world is that it's so ephemeral. For the most part, God seems to remain tantalizingly incognito. As Martin Wroe expresses it in his wonderful book *When You Haven't Got a Prayer*:[3]

> *The songwriter said,
> these are the days of miracles and wonders,
> but most times the signs are not so clear.
> Most days, we're alone,
> no voice from the heavens.
> The pages of your book are silent.*
>
> *Then, God,
> you're like a man painting street signs
> in a strange language,
> you're like the child showing her parents
> her drawing of a cow,
> which looks more like East Anglia.
> We can't understand the signs...
> and sometimes it seems like
> you're playing with us,
> that you don't want to be found out,
> that you're embarrassed or shy...*

The exception to this game of divine hide and seek is Jesus Christ; in him God has stepped out of the shadows and onto the main stage, where everyone can see. The most central Christian conviction is that when we look at Jesus, we are looking at God:

> *No one has ever seen God. It is God the only Son, who is close to the Father's heart, who has made him known. (John 1:18)*

That being the case, it becomes important to know something about this Jesus person. Apart from a few historical scraps, the main source of reporting about him is to be found in the four Gospels, and their collections of eye-witness accounts. These are reports of 'what we have heard, what we have seen with our eyes, what we have looked at and touched with our hands' (1 John 1:1). For us who are participants in history, Jesus represents the face of God by which we may discover what God is like.

Jesus the way to God

For most people, information about God is not enough. They want access to God, and rightly so. Web junkies will know how frustrating it is to come across a great site, which promises to have everything you are looking for, only to find that access beyond the front page is blocked. In order to open the site and be able to explore, you either have to pay some dosh or provide a password. Access is all-important, and it's no different with God. Bits of God, of course, are in the public domain. But the good stuff is only available through Jesus Christ.

Fortunately, Jesus is freely available to those wanting to sign up. There's no payment involved, apart from your whole life. Some people moan about Jesus being the means of access to God. They want God out there, completely user-friendly and without restriction. I'd like a Harley Davidson, but that's not the way things are. You want full access to God, you go through Jesus:

> *Jesus said to him, 'I am the way, and the truth, and the life. No one comes to the Father except through me. If you know me, you will know my Father also.' (John 14:6, 7)*

In another place, Jesus talks about himself as being the gate (John 10:9). Gateways are something that computer buffs are familiar with. Jesus is the gateway to God. The good news is that access through this particular gateway is very easy to arrange.

In the name of God

One of the reasons all this is so important is because people keep coming up with impersonations of God, and God gets fed up about it. The Nazi SS had the legend 'God with us' on their belt buckles. The American dollar has 'In God we trust' inscribed on it. Mass-murderers are wont to inform the public that 'God told me to do it'. Hollywood actors thank God when they should be thanking their plastic surgeons. Insurance companies hold God responsible for natural disaster, and point clients in that direction for recompense. And all of us know instinctively that whenever things go wrong, it's God who's to blame.

Contrary to popular belief, the Bible is not about whether God exists or not. It's about who God is, in the face of all these false representations. The fact is that throughout history, people have projected on to God what they see in themselves. It's like men who go searching for a woman to marry who resembles their mother. We have been guilty of inventing God to serve our own purposes. This is what's called idolatry, and really, it's silly.

Pretty much all the wars that have been fought have pulled the name of God into the act at some point or other. With opposing sides offering prayers, and confident that God is on their side, one can only assume there is something of a divided personality in the divine psyche. In many historical instances, including those of Hitler's Germany and South Africa, God has been invoked as the Great Racist. The power-holders in these states have been quite comfortable with the notion that God has ordained them to racial superiority. A chaplain offered God's blessing on the air crew who were about to depart on the mission to bomb Hiroshima in 1945. Can this God be the same one worshipped by Francis of Assisi and Mother Teresa?

I don't think so. Just because the name of God is used or scraps of scripture quoted, there is no reason to assume that God is in any way involved. But it does become important to sort out the real thing from the imposters. Although there is no shortage of people who claim first-hand experience of God, and seem to be on very chummy terms, their conflicting reports engender confusion if not cynicism. That's why it's important to check out God's own site for yourself. It's like looking up John Lennon on the net. You might get something like 21,187,145 hits, all containing information with varying degrees of accuracy. But all of them would pale into insignificance if you knew that Lennon was maintaining his own site, which could be accessed.

Certainly God has seen fit to take issue with the false reports which inhabit religious imagination, by stepping forward in the person of Jesus. Because of that, we are able to pick God out from the suspects' lineup down at the local Deity Parade. We discover a set of criteria by which to evaluate claims of divine presence. Once you've looked into the face of God through the image provided by the front page, you're more able to recognize the signs of God lurking in other places. Jesus is God's self-communication, and there's nothing quite like the horse's mouth. Of course, all of this requires that we get a good look at Jesus, and that's not always as simple as it might appear.

Plastic replicas

At some point in time, the people who had knocked around with Jesus started to write down their stories and memories. Up until that point in time, it had been enough to sit around and tell their tales to any who would listen. But as the word spread, bizarre things began to happen. People began to make things up about Jesus, and add in bits and pieces which they thought were more interesting. Anyone who has played Chinese whispers will know how this works. Over time, it started to get out of hand. False impressions were being given of Jesus. When you start with the proposition that Jesus represents God, then distortion is serious stuff. So the original witnesses issued their authorized statements. We call them the Gospels.

The process of misrepresenting Jesus didn't stop there, however. Throughout history, there has been a steady queue of charlatans manipulating the image of Jesus in order to advance their own ends. If we had to rely on a chain of reporting, we would be in serious trouble. Amazingly, against all odds, we still have access to the original records of those first witnesses. The picture of Jesus thrown up on the front page of scripture is not a bad likeness. The model has been constructed on the basis of profiles from four different perspectives. By using this holographic image, we can dismiss the plastic replicas which continue to be promoted as the real thing.

Jesus the nice guy

Those who don't know much about Jesus, and some of those who do, offer the generous interpretation that he was a nice guy. By which they seem to mean that he was kind to hedgehogs and always sent flowers to Mary on Mother's Day. On this understanding Jesus talked of love and peace, and was a sort of Middle Eastern hippie. His main contribution to society was the golden rule, which no one can quite remember, and it might actually have been Gandhi or someone who said it anyway. He is the sort of chap you can admire, and offer to schoolchildren as the epitome of good cricket and fair play.

In fact the Gospels tell us that Jesus wasn't particularly nice at all. He told his mother off, split up families, called people nasty names, damaged property and generally caused uproar. He wandered around Palestine with a bunch of no-hopers, causing trouble wherever he went. He was a zealot and an enthusiast. No parent would want their child running off with such a man. He consorted with people who were, frankly, not quite respectable, and had something of a reputation as a glutton and a drunkard. In the end, the civic authorities had him put to death as a rebel, a blasphemer and a heretic. All this we know from the Gospels; if it weren't true, they surely would not have wanted to record it.

Jesus the magician

Some people are keen on Jesus as a miracle-worker. They tout him as a cosmic magician, who had the power to solve any problem. According to this school, Jesus walked around with a visible glow emanating from the divine energy which was within him. He could produce wine out of water, a banquet out of a few fish, and no doubt rabbits out of hats if need be. His main mission in life was the eradication of disease, demons and disability. The special power which he had is now available to his followers, who are able to pull off similar feats. Do you have cancer or lumbago or a short leg? Jesus will fix it for you! All you need is faith, and a small donation to the expenses of our mission.

There is no doubt, on the evidence of the Gospels, that Jesus performed miracles. They were an accompaniment of his message, wherever he went. But the healings and exorcisms were signs: indicators of who Jesus was. Unfortunately attention tended to drift from Jesus and his teaching to the goodies which were spin-offs of his ministry. At one point Jesus describes the throngs as an 'evil generation' for demanding signs (Luke 11:29). He tells them off for being more interested in a free feed than doing the will of God (John 6:26). And we learn that despite the miracles which he performed, people did not believe in him (John 12:37). Following Jesus may produce miracles; it would seem that performing miracles does not produce followers.

Jesus the guru

From fairly early in the history of Christianity, there were those who wanted to see in Jesus a mystical bearer of religious secrets. They looked for special codes in the things that he said, and explained that there were many hidden things about his life which could only be revealed to the truly spiritual. And it just so happened that the people telling this story were among the enlightened. Still today there are those who would like to make Jesus into an Eastern guru, a dispenser of wisdom and deep teaching. He is the ascetic master, with special knowledge to impart. Only those in the know are 'real' followers of Jesus; the rest are like dumb sheep.

In point of fact, Jesus does not make a very good guru. His close friends report him as one who enjoyed life to the full, spending most of his time around the dinner table eating and drinking with the low-life. His teaching, though often profound, was only one part of a very active life and ministry. Unlike traditional gurus, it's not possible to separate what Jesus had to say from what he did. Sometimes he got angry, and acted in a distressingly un-guru-like manner. When it came to dying, he neglected to accept it with equanimity and serenity, but struggled against the prospect, and died shouting out in anguish and despair. Perhaps he should have taken up yoga.

Jesus the patron

Then there are those who are not so keen on following Jesus, and would prefer Jesus to follow them. They see him as a sort of religious patron of their lifestyles, who will provide them with a bit of extra blessing if they hang his picture on the wall. Some are convinced that Jesus' main concern was prosperity, and that he wants all of his people to enjoy a little bit of heaven in the here and now. On this view of things, a few mansions and limousines are signs that Christ is blessing his chosen ones. Prosperity, health and funny haircuts seem to be the fruit of the Spirit. Jesus once made fish into a feast; now surely he will make your faith into a fortune. Only believe, brothers and sisters!

Given the Gospels, it is hard to see how anyone could be audacious enough to advance this interpretation. Jesus certainly has a lot to say about money, but it's mostly about how following him means losing it. He counsels people to shift their focus from gold to God, and sees wealth and possessions as potential barriers to discipleship. The thrust of his message has to do with giving things up and trusting God. It seems that following Jesus means leaving behind a lot of the stuff which was previously considered to be precious and important. If there is any reward available, it is not to be found on this side of history. Jesus starts off in a respectable middle-class family, and ends up poor and abandoned, a criminal. Not much promise there for wannabees.

The real thing

So much for the cheap replicas. They wouldn't be such a problem if it weren't that their promoters ransack scripture in support of their chosen image. In parody of the creation story, they make God in their own image. There are all sorts of stories about God in the Bible, some of them representing weird ideas, and they provide ample material for anyone trying to stitch together a god of their own design. Somewhere in scripture you have to make a stand; find a centre and a perspective by which to evaluate the rest of the stories. That centre is to be found in the Gospels, which give us access to Jesus. As the image of God, he is (with all due deference to Coke) the Real Thing.

On the basis of the Gospels, we would have to evaluate some material in the Bible as sub-Christian. So, for instance, when the psalmist suggests, 'Happy shall they be who pay you back what you have done to us! Happy they shall be who take your little ones and dash them against the rock!' (Psalm 137:8, 9) we would not want to see this as God's optimum strategy for human coexistence. Rather we need to offer the correction as suggested by Jesus:

> *But love your enemies, do good, and lend, expecting nothing in return. Your reward will be great, and you will be children of the Most High; for he is kind to the ungrateful and the wicked. Be merciful, just as your Father is merciful.*
> (Luke 6:35, 36)

In Jesus we discover God, and are able to recognize distortions. What then do we find by scanning the front page of God's site?

God is for us

Contrary to popular belief, God does not consider humans to be some form of low scum polluting an otherwise passable universe. Nor is God hanging about waiting for the opportunity to inflict suffering or punishment on anyone who is naughty. In Jesus we discover the deep and abiding love of God for humanity. In his weeping over Jerusalem, in his compassion for the crowds, in his anguished cry from the cross—'Father, forgive them; for they do not know what they are doing' (Luke 23:34)—we see the hunger of God for relationship and friendship. God made humanity, and like an anxious parent is waiting for a return of the love which is unconditionally extended.

God is with us

We are not alone in the universe, and I am not talking UFOs here. Much as God may keep a relatively low profile, the history of humanity carries the abiding fragrance of God's presence. In Jesus, God steps out of the shadows, coming to us in a way we can relate to. At the centre of the incredible story of the Gospels is the notion that God has turned up in human life in order to be close to us. Everyone wants to find God:

> Philip said to him, 'Lord, show us the Father, and we will be satisfied.' Jesus said to him, 'Have I been with you all this time, Philip, and you still do not know me? Whoever has seen me has seen the Father.' (John 14:8, 9)

In Jesus God comes to us, and reassures us that the basis of that approach is love.

God suffers us

Not in the sense of reluctantly putting up with tiresome children that you'd rather be shot of, but as a parent who finds that their life is inextricably bound up with their children. God watches, grieves and suffers with us and for us. Human existence is painful. In Jesus we discover that God does not cause pain, or allow pain, or dismiss pain; God bears pain. The Gospels are dominated by that part of Jesus' story in which he is tried, tortured and crucified. A Roman centurion, seeing Jesus die, was able to say, 'Truly, this man was God's Son!' (Mark 15:39). The earliest witnesses understood that his death was 'for us'. Through Jesus has come the understanding that God's strategy is to draw pain into the divine heart, and there baptize it in love.

God loves us

Centuries of abuse mean that the bald statement sounds trite. It is not. Those three words represent the beating heart of scripture. They would remain just words were it not for the fact that Jesus lived, died and rose among us. Now they have become humanized and enfleshed and made present in Jesus, the Word of God.

> *God's love was revealed among us in this way:*
> *God sent his only Son into the world that we might*
> *live through him. (1 John 4:9)*

If it were not for Jesus, we might not have understood. Were it not for the Gospels and their eye-witness accounts of Jesus, we might have forgotten. Were it not for the Bible, and its preservation of those first stories, we might have been misled. The above four characteristics of God are brief and inadequate. But they're not bad things to know, and provide a matrix against which to test claims about God.

#4

Reality Check

It's a weird thing, but sometimes when you're sitting in front of your VDU, you catch a reflection of your own face off the screen. God's home page does something similar. Not only does it introduce you to the big G, but you also come face to face with yourself. And the image is brutally honest. The Bible is a mirror. As has been said, 'A donkey looking into it shouldn't expect to see a saint looking out.'

Our time has been described as the age of narcissism. Narcissus is the guy who looks into the pool of water and falls in love with his own reflection. If he had looked into scripture, he would have seen quite a different image. The Bible reflects what is on the inside. Perhaps that is another reason why it is waning in popularity. A generation that spends so much time and effort on contemplating the outward appearance doesn't want to be reminded of what lies behind it.

The loss of a sense of eternity seems to have produced a society which demands the benefits of the afterlife here and now. Everyone is obsessed with appearance, health, fitness and youth. Age has lost its dignity and death is treated as a nasty rumour. Perhaps the weirdest expression of this is the group known as the Physically Immortals. Hailing from California (where else?), this movement asserts that people only die because they expect to. Refuse to admit the possibility of extinction, and it won't happen to you. The group has yet to establish life membership.

A New Zealand novelist by the name of Janet Frame has a wonderful short story entitled 'Journey through the Human Heart'. It concerns a teacher who takes her class of schoolchildren to a scientific exhibition which is, literally, a journey through the valves and ventricles of the human heart. The children's cruel jibes and baiting of the teacher bring about an emotional crisis for her. She becomes aware of issues in her life that have been kept under wraps. Finally she breaks down and runs out on her pupils, the journey through the human heart proving too painful to bear.

Humans are masters at the art of self-deception. We are able to create masks and personae for ourselves at will, with which we deceive not only others, but also ourselves. Dishonesty and deception are not conducive to spiritual growth, however. From time to time, it is helpful to take a good long look in the mirror of scripture, and see ourselves as we really are. While such a journey through the human heart may induce horror, it also invokes the honesty which is the beginning of all wisdom.

Virtual reality

For most of us, virtual reality is not a new discovery. It is what we have been constructing and living in throughout our lives. The superstructure consists of those gentle lies which we adopted in preference to the stark truth. At an early age we discover what it is that people expect from us, and set about providing the appearance of it. More significantly, we design and decorate images of ourselves which are presented to the world as virtual identities. The hollowness behind the mask is easily concealed.

Scripture contains bits and pieces associated with God's dealings with humanity over thousands of years. It also makes the bold assertion that our humanity itself is the result of God's creative endeavour. All of which adds up to a reasonably thorough understanding of the condition known as humanity. On the rock of the Bible our evasions, projections and justifications shatter. It is like returning home to an ancient grandmother, who in two loving sentences can pierce the carefully crafted illusions by which we have survived for years. The Bible doesn't leave much room for hiding, unless you hide from the Bible itself.

A reality check is as important for the soul as a safety check is for a vehicle. Regular confrontation with the image reflected in the pages of scripture disperses the mists of deception and enables honest navigation for the spiritual journey. It may be well to survey some of the contemporary distortions which the Bible pierces.

We're all basically nice people

I like to be liked. I want other people to think what a thoroughly nice guy I am. I sometimes convince myself that I'm basically a good bloke. I don't rape, kill or pillage, or at least I haven't yet. Most other people are like me—that is, basically nice. There's just a few bad apples who cause all the trouble in the world. Eventually we'll educate them as well, and then the planet will be a thoroughly decent place to live.

In the face of this, the Bible asserts: 'The heart is devious above all else; it is perverse—who can understand it?' (Jeremiah 17:9). In other words, we may be able to fool ourselves, but that doesn't cut much ice with God. In the teaching of Jesus (Matthew 5:21–48), he makes it clear that even those of us who look fairly respectable on the outside are guilty of mayhem when it comes to the unseen inner life. In our hearts, we regularly commit murder and wreak vengeance on our enemies. And as scripture reminds us, '… the Lord looks on the heart' (1 Samuel 16:7).

Some years ago I made a pilgrimage to the concentration camp of Dachau, just outside Munich. It too was like a mirror. As I looked into that dark chasm of the psyche, I became aware of what humanity was capable of. More to the point, I recognized what I was capable of. Genocide lurks within the cavern of my heart, awaiting the right circumstance to emerge. Other people are just like me. Whatever humans have done, we all are capable of doing. Evil does not exist only in the world. It is present in our hearts.

We're all basically nasty people

The equal and opposite mistake is to imagine that there's nothing good in us. Not so popular these days, this view was beloved of many Calvinists who delighted in being wretched reprobate worms, and treating others as such. The corollary of this attitude is to expect the worst from people and prepare yourself for it. Trust neither yourself nor anyone else. Do unto others before they do unto you. Humanity consists of beasts who have adopted the habit of standing upright, but beasts they remain.

At www.God, however, we learn the outrageous story that we have been made in the image of God (Genesis 1:27). Whatever the locus of that image may be is not important. It is enough to listen to Mozart, or look on Van Gogh, or read Gerard Manley Hopkins to know that there is something of God within humanity. The psalmist says it this way:

> *What are human beings that you are mindful of them, mortals that you care for them? Yet you have made them a little lower than God, and crowned them with glory and honour.* (Psalm 8:4, 5)

It is a useful approach to adopt with people; to look for that of God which may be within them.

The assumption of badness is something of a self-fulfilling prophecy. It is also, like the assumption of sole goodness, hopelessly simplistic. Scripture acknowledges that humanity is more complex than that. There is the insightful depiction of the creation of humankind in Genesis 2, in which God scoops up a handful of dust and breathes the divine life into it. Understanding humanity as a mixture of mud and the breath of God is not a bad starting point.

Life is about getting ahead

This principle seems to be the touchstone of orthodoxy in Introductory Economics: *To Each According to their Greed*. According to such wisdom, the highest end of humanity lies in the accumulation of stuff and the advancement of career. She who collects the most boys wins, or words to that effect. All of us recognize material goals as being inadequate incentives, but in the meantime our lives are too busy in pursuit of them to have time to worry. Money and power may not satisfy, but they fill in time while you're waiting for enlightenment.

Scripture comes from quite a different perspective. According to Micah 6:8, the highest end of humanity is: 'to do justice, and to love kindness, and to walk humbly with your God'. Relationship with God is the all-important concern of existence. Jesus reduces the entire content of God's home page to two aims: loving God and loving the people around us (Matthew 22:34–40). He counsels attention to these objectives, rather than to lives of consumption:

> *Therefore do not worry, saying, 'What will we eat?' or, 'What*
> *will we drink?' or, 'What will we wear?' For it is the Gentiles*
> *who strive for all these things; and indeed your heavenly*
> *Father knows that you need all these things. But strive first for*
> *the kingdom of God and his righteousness, and all these*
> *things will be given to you as well. (Matthew 6:31–33)*

Underlying scripture is the recognition that we have been made to be
in relationship with God, and that without it there will always be a
yawning gap that nothing else will fill. As Augustine had it, 'Our
hearts are restless until they find their rest in you, O Lord'.[4] Looking
into the mirror of the Bible reminds us how empty our lives are when
we substitute wealth or prestige for the love of God:

> *For you say, 'I am rich, I have prospered, and I need nothing.'*
> *You do not realize that you are wretched, pitiable,*
> *poor, blind, and naked. (Revelation 3:17)*

This is all there is

If there is nothing more to human existence than these seventy-odd
years scratching a living out of the concrete jungle, then indeed (to
quote the voluble Bible) 'let us eat and drink, for tomorrow we die'
(1 Corinthians 15:32). To assume that there is nothing beyond death
is to live life with desperation, in the attempt to squeeze as much into
it or out of it as possible before the curtain falls. Many people appear
to be doing just that, constantly checking to see if they're having fun
yet, and gnawed at by the belief that nothing which they love will last.

In the eyes of scripture, this is an appallingly limited view of human
life. The Bible sets our existence against the backdrop of a purposeful
creation, in which death is significant, but unable 'to separate us from
the love of God in Christ Jesus our Lord' (Romans 8:39). Life in God,
as envisaged in scripture, is life without limit, abundant life (John
10:10). Rather than attempting to preserve our lives from threat, and
make the most of every moment, we must learn to let go of it.

> *For those who want to save their life will lose it, and those*
> *who lose their life for my sake, and for the sake of the gospel,*
> *will save it. For what will it profit them to gain the whole*
> *world and forfeit their life? (Mark 8:35, 36)*

The odd thing is that those who increase the margins of life by looking beyond the full stop of death are not, as we might expect, too heavenly minded to be of any earthly use. An appreciation of the height and depth and breadth of life rather leads to treating it as sacred, and therefore valuing experiences and celebrating them. It is an open-handed approach to life, which obviates the need to grasp at or cling to people or events. From such a perspective, the lifestyles of contemporary hedonists appear frenetic and dull. There is more to life, as someone has said, than meets the I.[5]

It's not my fault

Freedom may be just another word for nothing left to lose, or it may be an excuse for refusing to take responsibility. Criminal trials are amusing in their hunt for causative factors in the commission of the crime. If an alcoholic father or a period of depression or an argument with a girlfriend can be unearthed, then these are paraded by the defence as emblems of innocence. Politicians will exude offensive matter *ad nauseum*, without once coming near admitting responsibility for any of the consequences of their decisions. Blame and denial are the instruments used for many a Houdini-like escape. It seems that nothing is anybody's fault these days.

In the early chapters of Genesis (which are scripture's reflections on what is important in life), there is the amusing tale of the tree, the snake, and Adam and Eve (Genesis 2:9–17, 3:1–24). The facts were that the Tree of Life was off limits to our two progenitors and that, despite this fact, the two of them had been tucking into its fruit. In this alone we learn something significant about human nature—that which is forbidden will always be attractive. But there is even more revealed when God calls the pair to account: Adam blames Eve, and Eve blames the snake. Unfortunately, God seems determined to sheet home responsibility where it belongs.

After their misdeed of eating from the tree of the knowledge of good and evil (run that past your Jungian spectacles), Adam and Eve 'hid themselves from the presence of the Lord God among the trees of the garden' (Genesis 3:8). They went into hiding because they knew they had done wrong. Today you have to fight for a place among the bushes. But God of course was not fooled. 'But the Lord God called to the man, and said to him, "Where are you?"' (v. 9). God asks still. There is no place of hiding from the Spirit of God (Psalm 139).

A further attempt to avoid facing the music occurs in Genesis 4: 1–16. Here Cain bumps off his brother Abel in a fit of jealous rage. When God shows up, wanting to know what has happened to Abel, Cain gives the response which has become a classic excuse in the English language: 'Am I my brother's keeper?' On this evasive line the entire ideology of economic rationalism relies, in presumption of a negative answer. God is uncooperative, informing Cain: 'Listen: your brother's blood is crying out to me from the ground!' Let this be the epitaph for those in our own world who discount social responsibility.

Religious games

It is not only for those outside the church that the Bible serves as a reality check. Many who inhabit the halls of religion have adapted their evasive strategies to give them an ecclesiastical edge. The temptation for people who have access to scripture is to use it in such a way that it has no effect on them (see 'Living with a Tiger'). Religious games are harder to spot, because they use the language and symbols of faith, while doing their best to circumvent the need for it. But people have been trying to pull the wool over God's eyes for millennia, and the Bible exposes religious games for what they are.

Hide and seek

The best possible place to hide from God is in a church. Because you're there, singing hymns and choruses, arranging flowers and generally making a nuisance of yourself, people assume you're relating to God. You can use religious language with dexterity and ease, and generally give off an odour of piety. Everyone will marvel at your spirituality, and leave you in peace. Some very effective atheists and materialists hang out in the church, without fear of discovery. They can fool the punters, but scripture has their number.

For many years in America, Presidents of every shape, size and conviction have laid claim to personal faith. I have no direct knowledge to suggest that their church-going is anything other than genuine, but it does at times seem difficult to reconcile with various developments in the public policy area. Some irredeemably cynical observers might suggest that the Evangelical credentials of presidential hopefuls are more to do with capturing a certain segment of votes than any genuine conversion. And on a more sinister level, recent criminal convictions suggest that the community of faith has attracted its share of covert sex offenders.

Lying low in the church is what the Bible speaks of as 'holding to the outward form of godliness, but denying its power' (2 Timothy 3:5). Jesus warns the Pharisees in the words of Isaiah: 'This people honours me with their lips, but their hearts are far from me' (Matthew 15:8). In another place he informs religious fugitives: 'Not everyone who says to me, "Lord, Lord," will enter the kingdom of heaven, but only the one who does the will of my Father in heaven' (Matthew 7:21). Not much hope there—from scripture's perspective, spiritual frauds stand out like teetotallers in a brewery.

I'm the king of the castle

One of the favourite games of the playground is climbing to the top of anything that happens to be around, and declaring, 'I'm the king of the castle, and you're a dirty rascal.' The resultant sense of superiority is ample reward for the effort involved. The church has its own version of this game, in which players compete to establish who is the most spiritual among them. The losers, by definition, are the 'dirty rascals', or in religious jargon, 'sinners'. Sometimes a whole congregation will ascend to the highest accessible point, from which they pronounce everyone in sight (except themselves) to be sinners.

Jesus tells a story against this game (Luke 18:9–14). It concerns a highly respectable man, a veritable pillar of the church, who went to the temple to pray. He found himself alongside a vulgar, dissolute reprobate of a man, who shouldn't have been seen dead in a place of worship. Turning up his nose, the churchman prayed to God: 'Lord, I thank you that I'm not like other poor specimens of humanity— thieves, rascals, adulterers, or even like this sorry sinner beside me. I give to the church and follow the church calendar.'

Meanwhile, the no-hoper alongside him refused even to look up, simply beating his breast and crying out, 'God, be merciful to me, a sinner.' This man, says Jesus, was welcomed into the heart of God, whereas his smarmy religious companion excluded himself through his pride. Summing up, Jesus declared, 'all who exalt themselves will be humbled, but all who humble themselves will be exalted.' Salvation lies in coming down from the castle, and owning up to being a rascal. Sometimes I worry that this message has not got through.

This game is played with great enthusiasm in some Christian circles, and is a variant of 'spot the sinner'. Participants, who are invariably good churchgoing folk, take it upon themselves to give God a bit of assistance in the tracking down of sin. With meticulous care, they conduct lengthy unsolicited examinations of other people's lives in a ceaseless hunt for unrighteous peccadilloes. Experienced players can spot a swear word at 200 paces, or sniff illicit substances on breath even after the ingestion of many mint lollies. Such thorough examination proceeds only in one direction, and has the effect of confirming the instigator in their own superior status.

The Bible will have none of this. Jesus, as usual, spoils what is otherwise a perfectly enjoyable pastime. He has the effrontery to accuse players of hypocrisy:

> Why do you see the speck in your neighbour's eye, but do not notice the log in your own eye? Or how can you say to your neighbour, 'Let me take the speck out of your eye,' while the log is in your own eye? You hypocrite, first take the log out of your own eye, and then you will see clearly to take the speck out of your neighbour's eye. (Matthew 7:3–5)

It is clear that Jesus doesn't understand the rules at all—the spying is only supposed to happen in one direction.

In a famous incident in which some good religious people have come across a woman who has been frolicking in a veritable thicket of sin, Jesus once again ruins the fun. The righteous crowd was about to enact the appropriate punishment on the sinful and adulterous hussy, which happened to be death by stoning. Jesus utterly takes the fun out of it by suggesting, 'Let anyone among you who is without sin be the first to throw a stone at her' (John 8:7). It is tempting to describe him as something of a spoilsport.

Charades

Everybody loves to pretend to be something they're not. Acting out different roles is a healthy and imaginative exercise. Sometimes, however, religious people take things a little too far, and begin to act out the religious life for the benefit of others. This has the advantage of giving the outward impression of deep devotion and religious authority, while preserving one's real identity untouched by the intrusive demands of God. Good religion is amongst the best theatre in town, and it's not surprising that those who have the lead roles come to enjoy the adulation of the crowds.

I recently attended a very high church service while in Melbourne, Australia. It was an exceedingly fine performance. The robed choir reached their top notes with ease, the censer was swung in elaborate patterns and all the readings were provided in well-modulated tones. Unfortunately it was nothing much more than a performance. It seemed for all the world like a meeting of the Society for the Preservation of Sixteenth-Century English Culture, all the more bizarre in a former colony of convicts. There seemed little acknowledgment that there was any spiritual reality beyond the words which were being intoned.

By now you will be expecting that scripture will poke holes in this innocent pastime, and you are right. The Bible seems to want to maintain that people are required to be honest and transparent in their relationship with God. Jesus (no wonder they had to take him out of the game) suggests unsympathetically that the religious leaders 'do not practise what they teach' (Matthew 23:3). He proceeds to attack them for performing their religious obligations with an eye to the audience, loving to dress up in fancy clothes and having everybody kow-tow to them (Matthew 23:5–7).

The alternative, suggested by Jesus, is to conduct our spiritual lives pretty much in secret (Matthew 6:1–18). While presumably this may be just as effective, it is not nearly as entertaining or enjoyable. If nobody knows how pious you are, it seems that the game is not worth the candle.

Tag

Tag is probably the most common game in the whole of the playground. Whenever someone is made 'it', they run around in mad circles trying to catch someone else who they can tag and designate 'itness' to. The worst possible thing is to be left as 'taggee' when the bell rings and playtime is over, for then you have to sit with this status for an unendurable period. The object, then, is to shift attention off yourself and on to someone else just as quickly as you can. It is a game readily understood and played with great frequency in religious circles. In this setting, being 'tagged' means having the direct attention of God upon yourself. The trick is to shift it as quickly as possible off yourself and on to someone else.

Once again, Jesus feels compelled to stick his oar in and bring such innocent playfulness to a grinding halt. He counsels people to stick with their own journey, and to refrain from either passing on responsibility or worrying about the fate of others. It is summed up in his baseline injunction, 'Do not judge' (Matthew 7:1). In other words, get your nose out of the spiritual affairs of others. When his friend Martha complains that her sister Mary is being lazy, Jesus tells her to mind her own business (Luke 10:38–42). When the disciple Peter wants to know what will happen to his colleague John, Jesus responds, '…what is that to you?' (John 21:23).

Fortunately, not many people take the Bible seriously, and so the game of spiritual tag proceeds unabated in most churches. Experienced parishioners are adept at applying any spiritual wisdom imparted in a sermon (which, admittedly, is rare) to someone else in the congregation who needs it. Nobody wants to be 'it'.

All of the games we play and masks we hide behind are attempts to avoid meeting up with the One who loves us, and knows us painfully well. That's our prerogative and choice as free human beings. But we shouldn't expect to practise our self-deceit in the dimension of God's home page. It is a reality-based zone, in which pretension, hypocrisy and concealment evaporate under the light of truth. People whose lives are ugly can convince themselves otherwise by avoiding mirrors. But once you have seen yourself as you are, it is difficult to forget. The reflective surface of the Bible is clear, clean and sharp, and serves to keep us in touch with reality.

A Multi-Story Faith

While dedicated churchgoers have been enduring the Sunday morning lecture on precepts of the faith, next door in the Sunday School room the Bible has been set free in the midst of the children. This is because it has been assumed that young people are not up to coping with the 'deeper principles' of scripture, and so must be coddled with biblical stories. And so, inadvertently, the kids dine out on the best part while the adults suck their lips on thin gruel. Which, in the crazy perspective of Jesus, is probably as it should be.

Some churches have as part of their morning worship a 'children's talk'. It is fascinating to note the change of dynamic when such an event occurs. A congregation that has been listless, resigned and dutiful may suddenly light up and display unmistakable signs of enthusiasm. If a good biblical story is told, as it often is, then the adults as well as the children will be rapt. Attention continues right up until the point of the 'moral' or 'lesson' of the story, at which point concentration wanders and shoulders slump again. It would do no harm for would-be preachers to examine the body-language of hearers during such events.

Story is the most ancient means of communication; a resilient vehicle for the transmission of history, culture and wisdom. From the time the first cave-dweller rocked up home to tell about the mammoth that got away, human beings have been trading in stories. It is reported that a famous Greek orator, Demades, once got up to speak to the assembled crowd in Athens. No one listened to him. The crowd was distracted, talking to each other, watching birds fly across the sky and no doubt attempting Mexican waves. Crestfallen, Demades stopped. After a moment's thought, he began again: 'Ceres one day began a journey in the company of a swallow and an eel...' Immediately all conversation stopped and he had undivided attention.

That's the power of story. It draws people in, and leads them on a journey to an unknown destination. Parents with fractious children have always understood the ability of a story to capture and settle imagination. Frankly, stories are almost impossible to resist. The Bible is full of them. It is difficult to comprehend why such a rich resource has fallen into disrepute, and been replaced by lecture in the halls of Christendom. It is the equivalent of Isaac selling his birthright for a mess of pottage. But, of course, that's another story...

A bag full of stories

The Bible is mostly stories. Sure, there's a bunch of other stuff in amongst it, but for the main part, it's story. There's good reason for that. A whole lot of it came into being before the advent of reading and writing. God's home page has its origins in an oral culture, where everything important had to be handed on from generation to generation by word of mouth. In order for that to happen, people had to store things in the memory, and the easiest format to enable this was that of story. The raw material was often shaped up in such a way that it could be told to people around the fire at night.

As we've already noted, scripture is a rag-bag of collected bits and pieces from the long historical journey of the people of God. In essence, it is the narrative history of the tribe—that multifarious and colourful band of sojourners who have had their lives tangled in the divine web. It is the touchstone of identity for such people; the story-book which reminds us who we are and what we're about. Not all biblical stories are about 'what happened'. Some of them are rather intended to remind us of 'the way things are'. The range and purpose of stories in the Bible is huge, but it may be useful to sample that range at various points.

A philosopher addressing this question might begin with the ontological proofs for the existence of God, which would have us gagging with boredom or snoring within minutes. Scripture prefers to chuck in a few stories. There's the story of a bloke called Abram, for example, who gets rattled by God and told to put ham in his name (perhaps a compensation for the fact that his descendants won't be allowed to put it in their stomachs). God tells Abraham to leave everything that is familiar, secure and comforting, and to strike off into the unknown in the hope of finding a better place. Already we start to get a picture of the sort of things that God is into.

Many adventures happen. You can read about them for yourself. But one incident in particular is a delightful part of the story. God, you see, tells Abraham that he's to be the father of a huge nation. There's only one problem. His wife, Sarah, is as barren as the surrounding desert. She literally can't conceive of having children. And she's ninety years old. She's not only post-menopausal, she's post caring about it. Abraham himself is cracking on at age ninety-nine. Prospects do not look good.

Then, one day, three strangers appear on the horizon. Abraham welcomes them and invites them to stop and chat and have something to eat. In true patriarchal style, he orders Sarah to whip up some scones for morning tea. While she's beating the batter in the tent, she overhears one of these strangers telling Abraham that he will return, and by that time Sarah will have more than a scone in the oven; she will have a son. This gets Sarah laughing fit to bust. 'Is that old ram Abraham going to get it up for a dried prune like me?' she chortles.

One of the strangers turns out not to be a stranger, but God in disguise. He's somewhat affronted by Sarah's cynicism, and repeats the promise. Well, lo and behold. We are mercifully spared the details, but Sarah's belly begins to swell in evidence of the endurance of God's word. When she finally gives birth to a son, Isaac (the beginning of the nation of Israel), she remembers her laughter, and the God who has caused it. Now it is not the bitter doubting laughter of a barren woman, but the joyous acknowledgment of One who can make the impossible happen. 'From now on,' she determines, 'everyone will laugh with me.'

So what does that tell us about God? You'll have to work it out for yourself. What do you think—I'm going to start explaining stories?

Where we came from

Everyone wants to know where they came from, from the curious infant to the ageing immigrant who begins a genealogical search. Most of the stories in the Bible have some relation to this question. They don't address it on the level of DNA or cell division. The Bible is not that superficial. One of my favourite stories in answer to the query is found near the very start of scripture (Genesis 2:4–8). You might like to use it next time a child asks you how people are made.

It seems that when God was into making things, he reached down to the earth (which was itself one of his recent works), and picked up a handful of dirt. Lovingly, he raised the dirt to his lips, and breathed into it his own life. Wonder of wonders, the soil was transformed into a human being, whom God placed tenderly in the garden which had been specially prepared. So that's where we humans come from. We are a mixture of mud and the breath of the living God. Which explains a lot, when you think about it.

Of course there's plenty of other stories, like the one about the people of God being in captivity in Egypt, and God stopping a murderer in his tracks in the desert, with the original episode of spontaneous combustion. About how he made of this stuttering fool the revolutionary leader who was to challenge the Pharaoh's power and free the people from oppression. And how they came at last to the promised land. But that's another story. Or the one that Christians love to tell, about the man rejected by everyone, who turned out to be God incarnate. And how he assembled a tribe of rascals, among whom we have found a home. All of these stories provide the same response. Where have we come from? We have come from God.

Why we do stuff

There's so many things in life to find out about, and there's no better aid to understanding this than having a toddler in the house. Some of the stories collected at the divine hosting service started life as answers to kids' questions. The most famous of these is the story behind the Passover feast. Each year, when the family is gathered around the table to celebrate Passover, the youngest child is to ask, 'Yo dudes, what's happening?' or words to that effect. That gives the old folk the opportunity to tell again the story of the escape from captivity, the trek through the desert, the hardship and rebellion, the heartache and eventual arrival. That's why we're doing this stuff, they are saying, because this is where we came from and this is who we are.

There are stories to go with places (why they're sacred) and stories to go with practices (why we need to do this). Stories about circumcision, stories about the tabernacle, stories about the ark, stories about kings and prophets, stories about the temple, stories about the law and stories about food. Not all of them provide very good answers to the question about why certain activities may be happening, but they do provide the opportunity for the retelling of another rambling tale which passes on valuable memories and builds identity. A function of belonging to the tribe is hearing and retelling the stories of the tribe.

With the advent of Christianity (the story of stories), there comes a whole new raft of narratives. Now there are stories about baptism, stories about the Lord's Supper, stories about miracles, stories about looking after people, stories about discipleship and stories about persecution. At the centre of them all is the story of that man Jesus, which is told over and over and over again. No one seems to get sick of it, and it never seems to lose its power to inspire and transform. 'Tell me the old, old story,' the hymn has it, and it is an injunction from the heart.

Some things to remember

Every now and again, people who live through experiences learn something from them. They try to pass some of this stuff on to others, to save them from unnecessary pain and danger. Scripture is chock-full of such handy hints for living. Although some of it is laid out in fairly prosaic and pedantic form (such as in the book of Proverbs), a lot of it is much more interestingly communicated through the medium of story. To take a well-known example, there's the tale of David and Goliath. You know the scenario: a king-size Philistine is making a mockery of the Jewish troops by challenging them to a fight.

Enter a slender shepherd by the name of David. His only qualification for battle is the stupidity of youth, and an undying faith that God is stronger than any opposition. Choosing five smooth stones (why this detail—what does it add to the story?), David uses his outrageous sling of fortune to down the brute. He has done it unaided, and with the simple resources he had at hand. That, and his trust in God. Whether the story happened in exactly this way or not is not the issue. It is a magnificent tale for when you're in a sticky situation and the odds are stacked against you. When taken to heart, it can change the way in which people perceive the world.

Which is what a lot of the stories in the Bible are about. You'll find accounts of rebellion, betrayal, doubt, tyranny, lust, hospitality, subterfuge, cunning, sacrifice, dislocation, loss, reconciliation, forgiveness, retribution and achievement. The stuff of human life is there, because over a few thousand years people get to face most of the issues which are likely to arise. Some of the stories serve as warnings; others as challenge; yet others as consolation. The Bible is a bag full of stories, and a bit of rummaging round will always find something useful and germane. As Jesus put it:

> *Therefore every scribe who has been trained for the kingdom of heaven is like the master of a household who brings out of his treasure what is new and what is old. (Matthew 13:52)*

Jesus and stories

Jesus had a few options open to him. He could, I suppose, have written a book. He might have started an institute of theological education. Perhaps he could have set up shop in the temple precincts, offering elucidation of the scriptures. Instead, he told stories. Stories which were so magical and engaging that still today they have the power to entrance, inspire, confound and transform their hearers. The parables of Jesus are highly stylized narratives at the high end of the story artform. With them he managed to excite the humble and silence the wise. If it weren't for God's home page, we would have no access to these wondrous tales.

The detractors of Jesus always wanted to get him into theological debate. These Doctors of Doctrine fancied themselves in any intellectual discussion of the faith, and wanted the opportunity to upstage this pretender by showing the logical inconsistency of his propositions. Jesus declined to play them at their own game, preferring instead to subvert the process. So, when a lawyer comes to him asking about eternal life, Jesus is aware that the man is trying to stitch him up. When the enquirer asks, 'And who is my neighbour?' (Luke 10:29), he is hoping for a prescriptive definition which will be up for scrutiny. Instead Jesus replies: 'A man was going down from Jerusalem to Jericho...'

Rather than delivering a ten-point sermon on 'The Precepts of Sanctification', Jesus says, 'Two men went up to the temple to pray...' (Luke 18:10). When he wants to teach people about the kingdom of God, he begins, 'A sower went out to sow...' (Matthew 13:3), or, 'Someone gave a great dinner...' (Luke 14:16), or yet again, 'There was a rich man who was dressed in purple...' (Luke 16:19). The crowds listened and were intrigued. Here was someone speaking of God in a way that was familiar and accessible, using the images of their everyday lives. They were drawn into the stories and found themselves led into the presence of God.

Jesus' use of stories was remarkable enough to provoke question from his disciples. When asked why he was so keen on them, he provided a mystifying answer:

> *To you it has been given to know the secrets of the kingdom of*
> *heaven, but to them it has not been given. For to those who*
> *have, more will be given, and they will have an abundance;*
> *but from those who have nothing, even what they have will be*
> *taken away. The reason I speak to them in parables is that*
> *'seeing they do not perceive, and hearing they do not listen,*
> *nor do they understand'. (Matthew 13:11–13)*

This seems a harsh response, as if his agenda was to confuse and mislead people. I suspect, however, that Jesus is referring to the special quality of stories which means that they conceal at the same time as they reveal. Only those whose hearts and imaginations are open are able to travel the full distance of the story. This form of communication is essentially dynamic, and leads to confrontation of the will rather than simply titillation of the mind.

Jesus was a storyteller *par excellence*. Let no one imagine that he simply opened his mouth and the stories appeared as if by magic. The stories he used show the evidence of careful crafting. They are based on observation of people and life, and reflect deep insight into both human nature and the reality of God. Such stories also reveal the application of creative imagination and forethought. Jesus has left us a rich heritage, both of the stories he used, and the art of storytelling as a means of communicating faith. Once again we must give thanks to the Bible for preserving and passing on this legacy to us.

Stories and how they work

It is time, I am convinced, for the people of God to reappropriate the biblical tradition of storytelling. It is hard to know how and why it has been allowed to languish. But the time and the age is ripe for its rediscovery. There is a lot to relearn, particularly in regard to the dynamic of stories and how they work. I have listened to people delivering stories as if they were quoting an encyclopaedia article, or dropping a stone tablet from a great height. To tell a story well is an art, and like any art, requires some knowledge of the discipline involved. So it may be useful to survey briefly some of the characteristics of story.

Stories begin in a shared reality

As all good teachers know, you must always begin where people are, if you are going to lead them somewhere else. It is no good calling to them from across the distance, and expecting your hearers to come to where you are. Firstly, you must travel to where they are. So it is that good stories always begin with the familiar. They contain places, people, situations and symbols which the listeners can immediately identify with. Look again at the parables of Jesus, and note how they are always located in the sphere of common experience.

Stories are open to all comers

With stories there is no segregation or entry requirement. Anyone can get on board. Unlike theology, there is no necessity for people to have an understanding of technical terms or a basic grounding in a particular discipline. Stories are so open and transportable, that in many cases you can find versions of the same story in each of the world's major religious traditions. As a rule of thumb, definitions exclude, while stories include. Each time something is spelled out more fully (as in a doctrinal statement), more people are shut out; whereas in a narrative, anyone who can relate to the events is drawn in.

Stories invite rather than instruct

In today's world, many people (me included) are sick of being lectured at. They do not want other people telling them what to do. The world is tired of moralizing lectures. It is the genius of stories that they adopt a quite different approach, even in dealing with the same issues. A story is an open journey, which people are free to join or opt out of as is their wish. In this way stories preserve people's individual dignity and freedom to choose, without crashing personal boundaries. Hearers are able to leave the narrative journey at any point of their choosing, and if they stay till the conclusion, they have no one to hold responsible other than themselves.

Stories operate at a number of levels

This is the point which Jesus was making about some people not understanding. Stories are deceptive. They seem, at one level, to be a narrative description of a series of events. At a much deeper level, however, they are often dredging up archetypal material from our psyches. The tale of *Moby Dick*, for example, is about more than whales. Bunyan's *Pilgrim's Progress* relies for its power on associations with the spiritual journey. With such stories, it is possible for some people to hear and not to hear at the same time. These are the sort of people who respond to a joke (which is after all a stylized story) with 'So?' Try as they may, they simply can't 'get it'. But for those who are 'hooked' by the story, it is capable of producing a significant internal transition.

Stories are vehicles of wisdom and spirituality

Because of the ambiguity of stories, they are marvellous vehicles for the simultaneous transmission and guarding of truth. For thousands of years, in a vast range of cultures, stories have been used for the selective passing on of tribal wisdom and spirituality. The treasure they contain is put out there for the discerning to receive and learn from, while the ignorant will pass by without awareness. This is the way in which God operates—never forcing people, but offering them the option of enlightenment if they are prepared to take it. Stories enable this to take place in tenderness and respect.

Stories have a certain rhythm

A well-told story is a meander from one point to another. Like any journey, there needs to be time for rest, time for making progress, time to be aware of danger and a time of arrival. It is helpful to be aware of the territory which a particular story must cover, and suit the pace appropriately. Spiritual tales, such as the ones Jesus told, at some point begin to dig below the surface for their hearers. At such times, there is a growing internal tension for people, and they will be tempted to avoid the psychic confrontation of drawing near the presence of God. It is as well for the narrator to note this dynamic, and allow for it.

Stories end without finishing

It is almost without exception wrong to provide an explanation for a story. That is to remove people's freedom of interpretation, and in many ways to restrict the space which God has for working through the story. Good stories end without finishing; their work continues in the life of the hearer. Many Christians find this frustrating. They want the truth to be spelled out unmistakably, and an end put to this infuriating ambiguity. I'm sure such people would have had the same feelings towards Jesus' original parables. One of my favourite stories for expressing narrative open-endedness is the following.

> *Once there was a very wise old man whose advice was sought from all corners of the kingdom. A young and jealous prince set out to humble the old man.*

> *'I will go to the sage with a bird in my hand, and ask him if it is alive or dead,' he decided. 'If he says it is alive, I will crush the bird in my hand and kill it. If he says that it is dead, I will open my hand and let it fly away.' The smug prince travelled many days, and eventually arrived at the old man's humble house. 'Tell me, old man, is this bird alive or dead?' he asked.*

> *The stooped prophet looked deep into the man's eyes, and said quietly, 'The answer lies in your hand.'*

Retelling stories from the Bible

A word of warning to the wise. The biblical stories have been around for a while. Simply retelling them in their original form can become just a tad predictable. In order to retain their freshness and bite, it helps to do a little bit of imaginative work on them. This is not tampering with them as much as preserving their initial vigour. The following is an example of what you might do: yet another retelling of the prodigal son, minus its conclusion.

OK. So there was this kid with the rich father. And he does the teenage angst thing, and he finds living at home a bit on the tight side, you know what I mean? So he goes to his old man, and he says 'Listen. One day I'm going to inherit all this, but by then I'll be too old to enjoy it. How's about you divvy up my share now, and I'll take off and leave you in peace?'

So his father cashes up the son's share of his inheritance, and the boy takes off into the distance. He does his overseas experience, you know? And he's got all this money, and there's people hanging off him, and it's party on, my man, party on. Life becomes a dizzy round of raging and substance-abuse and morning-afters to die for, literally. Until one day he blows the last of his bank balance, and reality descends like a hunk of concrete. For some reason his friends are nowhere to be found.

So he gets himself a job on a pig farm, trying to keep ends together. Times are tough. He finds himself looking longingly at the pigswill, picking up the odd cabbage leaf to nibble on. And he has this sort of revelation thing. 'Man,' he thinks, 'the labourers back home live better than this. What am I doing grovelling around in the mud?' So he shoulders his pack and begins the long journey back home.

Many days later, he arrives on the front porch, hungry and dirty and tired. He bangs on the front door with a sense of anticipation. But there's no answer. So he knocks again, and still no answer. Again, and this time a window flies open upstairs and his father glares out. 'Ah, so it's you back again, is it? You look like something the cat dragged in. What's up? Run out of money, have we? Come home to sponge off the old man? After I gave you what was yours. Think I'm a soft touch, do you?'

A bit taken aback, the son goes, 'Father, I have sinned against heaven and before you…' But the only thing he hears is the window banging shut. He waits on the doorstep, and eventually the front door opens. His father looks at him and scowls.

'You're a disgrace, that's what you are, a bloody disgrace. I've
had a gutful of you. And where'd you get that tattoo? I suppose
I've got no choice but to take you in, seeing I'm your father. But
you're on trial for three months, and if I have one word out of
you, or you put one foot wrong, you're down the road,
you understand?

Nah, that's not the way it happened. In fact he was still walking up the road toward home, going over the story he's going to use, when he hears this huge 'Wahoo!' and sees a man running toward him. It sounds like his name that's being called, and he slowly understands that this is his father running toward him like a madman. With a swoop his father is on him, wrapping him up in a bear hug and crying. The son is dazed, and goes into the speech he's prepared. 'Father, I've sinned...' But his father cuts him off in mid-sentence, looks him in the eye and says simply, 'I know.' Both crying now, they make their way toward home. Once inside, the boy's father cracks a bottle of his best champagne, takes the steak out of the freezer, and rings round the neighbourhood to tell people there's a party on that night. 'My boy here was lost,' he says, 'maybe dead. But now I've found him and he's home to stay.'

Fire in the Bones

I once led a communion service in the rubble of a demolished building. It had been a hospital ward caring for the elderly. In its wards, people had been cared for and people had died. Many saw out their last days there, holding on to family members and telling their stories one last time. Some had been nursed to health, and looked back on the place with warm affection. But now it was a pile of bricks, knocked down to make way for a hospital carpark. One member of my congregation had been a senior physician in the block, another a staff nurse. They grieved the loss of the building, with all its rich memories. And so it was that on a Good Friday, we broke bread and poured out wine amidst the ruins.

We were a small band of worshippers, gathered in an unlikely setting. The atmosphere was enhanced by security guards, who prowled around us speaking into their radio-telephones. It seemed appropriate to the crucifixion we were remembering. By the end of the service, some people were moved to tears. We held on to each other, frail witnesses of a kingdom the world was not interested in. The piles of unloosed bricks seemed a symbol of the vulnerability of love to the machinery of efficiency. And then, as we were walking away, one of us spied something in amongst the rubble. He reached down and worked it free. In astonishment, he raised it so that we could all see.

It was a Gideon's Bible; mangled, crushed, dirty—but still miraculously intact.

It became for us a sign of hope. A hint that the message of God is remarkably resilient in the face of what seems overwhelming odds. In the popular imagination, scripture is a dusty relic, due to be buried under the detritus of the second millennium. But rumours of this demise are entirely exaggerated. God remains God, and the desire for self-communication in the divine heart still flares us out to embrace and singe us all. Set free from constraint, scripture retains the power to create and nourish life of the type which has no limit. God's home page is a gateway to torrential passion, wild idealism and brooding love. Let the technocrats do what they can to silence it; the voice of God will call until the end of time.

The Word and the Spirit

The Bible is not the Word of God, as we noted in chapter 3. It would be a terrible misrepresentation to imagine that the Word of God could be locked up within inky squiggles on a page. Or to suggest that a librarian could casually catalogue and shelve the self-communication of the Creator of all that is. No, the Bible is not in and of itself the Word of God. However, the good news is that the Bible may become the Word of God to us, in certain circumstances. As all cyber-junkies know, it is of little use to have web-browsing software on your computer, unless you have a connection. Without that interactive flow between server and browser, nothing is going to happen.

It is the Spirit who is able to transform a bound copy of the Christian scriptures into the Word of God, and the Spirit alone. God is a God of encounter, and prefers not to communicate in any detached or abstract fashion. To hear, to know, to see, to feel the Word of God, one must be in the presence of God. And that presence is mediated through God the Holy Spirit; that part of the Trinity which John V. Taylor has unforgettably named 'The Go-Between God':

> What makes a landscape or a person or an idea come to life
> for me and become a presence towards which I surrender
> myself? I recognize, I respond, I fall in love, I worship—yet it
> was not I who took the first step. In each such encounter there
> has been an anonymous third party who makes the

introduction, acts as a go-between, makes two beings aware of each other, sets up a current of communication between them... Christians find it quite natural to give a personal name to this current of communication, this invisible go-between. They call him the Holy Spirit, the Spirit of God.[6]

The Word of God is essentially life-giving. The wonderful story of the calling into being of creation in Genesis has God speaking the world into existence. The same description pictures the Spirit of God brooding over the waters (Genesis 1:2). From the beginning, the Spirit and the Word are linked. They work in partnership, and the evidence of their passage is life. The Spirit of God is the medium in which the Word of God takes shape, in the same way that air is the medium which carries our human communications. Without some such medium, in the presence of a vacuum, there is nothing but silence.

The Bible is useless without the Spirit. It is a car with flat tyres, a television with no power, a pencil without lead. You might use it to stand a flower pot on, or to fill out your bookshelves, or to add an air of sanctity to a disordered house; but without the Spirit it will simply be consuming space. It might be read from, memorized, studied, quoted and enshrined on posters over scenes from nature, but without the Spirit, it will be words floating in the breeze. The Spirit is the life-giving force of scripture; the midwife who opens the womb of the imagination. Under the brooding of the Spirit, the captive words of scripture become bearers of the divine presence. Let us consider some of the ways in which this transformation takes place.

Spirit as breath

In the wonderfully earthy and evocative language of Hebrew, the same word, *ruach*, means spirit, breath and wind. In many cases the precise meaning of *ruach* is not clear, and all the ambiguities and overtones of it are allowed full rein. The key to understanding is that Spirit is enlivening, as can be illustrated from a few biblical examples. In one which we have already considered, God takes the dirt from the ground in order to fashion humanity, and breathes life into it (Genesis 2:7). This breath is the breath of life, the spirit, the life of God, the evidence of life. By sharing something of the divine Spirit, God passes on life and breath to men and women.

In the book of Ezekiel, we find the prophet's vision of a valley of dry bones (Ezekiel 37:1–14). The setting is a barren valley, littered with sun-bleached skeletal remains. It is the epitome of death and desolation, a cemetery of hope. The question from God to Ezekiel is this: 'Mortal, can these bones live?' The prophet, in an answer which would qualify him for the diplomatic service, says, 'O Lord God, you know.' Ezekiel is then invited to deliver the word of the Lord to the bones, and to bring them to life by so doing. He faithfully preaches to the assembled bones, and is treated to a remarkable sight:

> So I prophesied as I had been commanded; and as I prophesied, suddenly there was a noise, a rattling, and the bones came together, bone to its bone. I looked, and there were sinews on them, and flesh had come upon them, and skin had covered them; but there was no breath in them. (Ezekiel 37:7, 8)

So the word of God has produced a remarkable transformation, but on its own it is not enough. The reconstructed bodies still have no breath, no life, no spirit. Ezekiel is instructed to prophesy again, this time to invoke the winds to breathe the breath of life into the dead. This time, life is granted. With the coming of life, breath, the Spirit, the great host of people is recreated.

From these instances we learn that the building blocks of life are not enough; they require the inspiration (breathing in) of the Spirit, the breath of God, in order for true life to ensue. In the same way the elements of scripture are not in themselves capable of doing the job. Only when the wind of the Spirit blows through them are they able to produce beating hearts. The birth of the church is associated with Pentecost (Acts 2:1–13). That was the day on which a tired and dejected group of Jesus' followers met together, only to be descended upon by the roaring wind of the Spirit. Prior to that time, everything was in place, as with Ezekiel's bodies; but until the Spirit blows, life does not begin.

Spirit as fire

When Moses encounters the presence of God, it is in the form of a fire (Exodus 3:1–6). Later, when the people of God are led through the wilderness, God appears to them as a pillar of fire (Exodus 13:21). Jeremiah speaks of the word of God within him in vivid terms: 'there is something like a burning fire shut up in my bones'

(Jeremiah 20:9). In the book of Hebrews, God is described as 'a consuming fire' (Hebrews 12:29). When the disciples meet the risen Christ on the road to Emmaus, they later question each other, 'Were not our hearts burning within us?' (Luke 24:32). And of course, in that pivotal event when the Spirit is pictured descending upon the church, fire touches the heads of the assembled followers (Acts 2:3).

There are many qualities of fire which the Spirit's presence evokes. Fire is wild and uncontrollable. Fire is warming, vibrant and passionate. In the presence of flames there is a sense of excitement. Fire is contagious and dangerous. It is difficult to contain. Likewise, the Spirit of God sears souls and inflames hearts. The same dancing liveliness of burning flames is to be found wherever the Spirit is at work. We are told that the bush which Moses saw burned, but was not consumed. The same bush which at another time he might have passed by without noticing, suddenly became for him the bearer of God's presence.

Perhaps it is in the same way that the same words of scripture, which at one time I tossed aside as being boring and irrelevant, later crackled with such intense heat that they left their branded mark on my soul forever. The Spirit of God sets the words of scripture alight for us, and they blaze with light. Like Jeremiah, we may well find that they become 'a burning fire shut up in my bones'. Those who find the Bible dull and prosaic have perhaps never seen the words lit up by the beacon of the Spirit in such a way that they beguile and compel. It is not surprising that they pass by unimpressed. Words only become the Word in the heat of encounter.

Spirit as ecstasy

The current drug of choice is Ecstasy. Those who use it report that they do so not simply to escape or get out of things, but to become more intensely aware of the connectedness of people and the universe. It is associated with dance parties and raves. Of course, it takes its name from the state which the dictionary describes as one of exalted joy or rapture. In its Greek derivation, ecstasy means literally 'to stand outside', and gives new meaning to the druggie term, 'out of it'. The early biblical prophets are sometimes described as 'ecstatic' prophets, because of the way in which they performed. Thus we read in 1 Samuel 10:10 of Saul, that 'the spirit of God possessed him, and he fell into a prophetic frenzy'.

Turning again to the day of Pentecost, we learn that after the Spirit's descent, the followers of Jesus acted so strangely that they needed to defend themselves against charges that they were drunk (Acts 2:15). They were ecstatic in the sense of having been lifted out of themselves and overwhelmed by the Spirit of God. Being around when God shows up can make it difficult to maintain an appearance of sobriety. There is enough similarity for Paul to exhort, 'Do not get drunk with wine,' but rather, 'be filled with the Spirit' (Ephesians 5:18). Not so much that the Spirit is a substitute drug, but that there are some similarities in the effects, as Frederick Buechner notes in his *Wishful Thinking*:

> [Wine] *makes the timid brave and the reserved amorous. It loosens the tongue and breaks the ice, especially when served in a loving cup. It kills germs. As symbols go, it is a rather splendid one.*[7]

Again, when the Spirit is inhaled, the word of God can bring delight and exuberance. The great discovery of the Pentecostals is that the journey with God has many similarities to a party. It can be a great deal more fun than many people make it out to be. There was a time in the days before I knew Christ when I was imprisoned in a Moroccan jail for drug use. Conditions were less than optimal. The day I was released from prison, I wandered around the streets as if I were seeing things for the first time. I'll swear the colours were brighter and the air sweeter. My heart was singing. In all probability, no one I passed on that day shared my joy. They were not participating in the experience of freedom. It is that sort of freedom, breathed through the scriptures by the Spirit, which causes ecstasy for those who taste it.

It is not only we who seek liberation, however. The Spirit yearns for the setting free of scripture, that it might resume its dance of engagement with humanity. Chapter 2 surveyed some of the ways in which the Bible is kept in captivity among well-meaning religious people. It is time to consider how scripture might be released, and through the power of the Spirit enliven us with breath, fire and ecstasy.

Setting scripture free

It is not people outside the church who are the enemies of scripture. By and large, they are disinterested. The real captors of the Bible are those who profess religious belief. It is they who can have a vested interest in subverting the power of scripture for change.

Freedom from institutional confinement

The defining image for me of institutional life is a long corridor lined with closed doors. It symbolizes some of the besetting sins of institutional life: the need for order, the desire to control, the feeling of remoteness, the hunger for survival, the abuse of authority and the managing of information. Institutions play many important positive roles as well; I just find it harder to remember them. Let us not underestimate the significance of the battle between the gospel of freedom and the dark side of institutional life. It was, after all, the conflict which ended in the cross of Christ.

Jesus got into trouble for driving to the heart of scripture, and revealing the petty evasions which interpreters of the law had constructed for themselves. The problem for those of us who live within the church is that the Bible is dangerous. It cuts through our justifications and pomposity, and nails us to the wall. This is not a pleasant experience. The Spirit and the Word in combination bring us face to face with the truth about ourselves and the truth about the way we live. If we were to take them seriously, we would have to accept that the poor are God's special ones, that experience in the faith is demonstrated through humility and service, that the task of the church is to give up its life for others, and that the road of discipleship frequently involves suffering.

You have to admit that on the face of it, this is not a good basis on which to run an institution. It's not surprising that canny people with an eye to the future have sought to, shall we say, interpret scripture in such a way that is more congenial to the survival of the enterprise. It takes a great deal of work, scholarship, cross-referencing and selective quoting, but eventually the message of the Bible comes out looking somewhat different. Now it teaches that poverty is a sign of laziness, that maturity in faith results in the ability to quote verses and to be elected to the deacons' court, that the task of the church is to preserve its purity against the heathen world, and that following Jesus often makes us healthy and wealthy and just a tad smug.

All this might sound a little cynical and unjust, until you read the words of Jesus in reaction to the religious people of his own time (which we have of course, courtesy of that most subversive of all works, the Bible):

> *The scribes and the Pharisees sit on Moses' seat; therefore, do whatever they teach you and follow it; but do not do what they do, for they do not practise what they teach. They tie up heavy burdens, hard to bear, and lay them on the shoulders of others; but they themselves are unwilling to lift a finger to move them. They do all their deeds to be seen by others; for they make their phylacteries broad and their fringes long. They love to have the place of honour at banquets and the best seats in the synagogues, and to be greeted with respect in the marketplaces, and to have people call them rabbi… All who exalt themselves will be humbled, and all who humble themselves will be exalted. (Matthew 23:2–7, 12)*

There follows a long litany of virulent complaint from Jesus, based on the accusation that the religious people have managed to manipulate the covenant of God to make it mean something quite different from what was intended (Matthew 23:13–36). They have done this through selective interpretation of scripture—through appearing to uphold the letter of it while debasing the intent. This is to use scripture to one's own ends; to leave the Spirit out of the loop. It is not a methodology which is merely of historical interest, but one which persists in the church today. There is an abiding temptation to possess the language of faith without encountering its source.

To break scripture free of institutional captivity is not an easy task. When my wife and I were studying at a seminary in Switzerland, she was asked to preach at an evening service of the local church, a largely student congregation. She took as her text '[Y]ou will know the truth, and the truth will make you free' (John 8:32). Her message was a celebration of the freedom that Christ has won for us; the ability to follow him without rules and regulations. After the service, the pastor came up to her in obvious consternation. 'You can't preach that to students,' he complained. 'You never know what they'll do with it. It's entirely too dangerous.' Yes, well, that's what the gospel is.

The mind is a fine human resource. It is one of the four elements of our existence with which we are invited to love God (Mark 12:30). The application of our minds to faith saves us from sinking into a swamp of emotion and superstition. Scholarship is a valuable resource to the church, and I have given a reasonable proportion of my life to the academic sphere. However, it must be said that under the sway of modernism, the mind has been given a position of dominance within faith which is undeserved, and which ends up distorting its value. The intellect is most useful at one step's remove from faith, where it can evaluate and inform. When it takes centre stage as the instrument of faith, it is inadequate to the task.

For many years in Christian history, the venue for academic life was that of the monastery. Here, the application of scholarship was set amidst a regular and disciplined life of prayer and devotion. Today, the locus and paradigm of theological education is that of the academy. Theology is studied as if it were no different a subject than chemistry or mathematics. The problem is that the use of the mind in relation to God is qualitatively different from its application in other areas. As soon as God is treated as a specimen to be examined, or scripture is regarded as simply one more text among others, there is an inevitable distortion.

Compounding the problem is the fact that most clergy are trained in such academic contexts. Along with the overt agenda of their course of study, they tend to pick up a 'hidden curriculum'. This teaches them that the preferred mode of communication is the lecture, that the prime interpreter of scripture is critical reason, that knowledge is superior to service, that competition is the means of advancement, and that scholarship is the greatest of all gifts to the church. Somewhere along the way, it is common for students to lose touch with such basics of Christian life as humility, compassion, prayer, sacrifice, forgiveness and kindness. It can take many years for a good congregation to retrain their minister in the fundamentals of the faith, and some never succeed.

Scripture has become a victim of cerebral captivity. In some Protestant churches, it is a rare thing to hear an uninterpreted word of scripture. And so the Bible dies the death of a thousand qualifications. Preaching is full of exegetical marvels, historical background and 'scriptural principles'. It is not uncommon for sermonizers to wallow in a couple of verses for a month, effectively robbing them of any connection they may have had with a wider context. So-called Bible studies become a means of speaking about scripture without it having any effect on the lives of those participating. Topics beloved of such studies are the meaning of the elements of the temple, or scriptural pointers to why Jesus might be turning up next week. They allow the appearance of discipleship without the reality.

God's home page is a resource for those who are on the journey of faith. Whenever it is taken in isolation from that journey, it becomes distorted. A story which I used in *Godzone* illustrates that beautifully. It concerns a great explorer who returned to her home village after a long expedition. The people welcomed her with enthusiasm. They wanted to know all about her adventures, and in particular about the mighty Amazon which she had travelled. But how could she speak of the feelings which had flooded her heart when she saw exotic flowers and heard the night sounds of the forests; when she sensed the danger of the wild beasts or paddled her canoe over treacherous rapids?

She said to the people, 'Go and find out for yourselves.' To guide them she drew a map of the river. They pounced upon the map. They framed it in their town hall. They made copies of it for themselves. They studied it night and day and became experts in interpreting the river. They knew its every turn and bend, they knew how broad it was, how deep, where the rapids and the waterfalls were. And yet, not one of them ever left the village to see the river for themselves.

Free from the dungeons of dogma

One of my favourite pieces of graffiti is, 'My karma ran over my dogma'. My dictionary reports that dogma is 'a system of doctrines proclaimed by ecclesiastical authority as true'. Clearly, it is closely associated with religious institutional life. Dogma is the religious equivalent of ideology; a set of ideas held with fanatic zeal to be true, and brooking no argument. Though on the surface the concern is with what is right and true, at a deeper level the issue is often one of power. Dogma is an attempt to control people by determining in what ways they are permitted to experience and interpret the world. Those who promote dogma generally have means of enforcing adherence to it.

Scripture is a vast resource. God's home page is such a broad eclectic agglomeration of material from different eras, contexts and cultures that it understandably contains a variety of perspectives. Thus, for instance, the first book of Samuel has voices arguing for and against monarchy, each passionate that their viewpoint is the correct one (compare 1 Samuel 8:10–18 and 10:17–19 with 1 Samuel 10: 1–7). Such contrast is too ambiguous for some who prefer their blacks clearly distinguished from whites. The solution is to make a personal selection from the scriptural array of 'good bits', and then to portray this selection as the real meaning of scripture; the interpretive key which makes sense of all the rest.

I've always been intrigued by the *Reader's Digest Condensed Version* of the Bible (it actually exists). This purports to cut out all the boring bits for the benefit of the reader. The interesting part, of course, is what material is tossed. The same procedure underlies dogmatic ventures. Dogma is built around the equivalent of a personal selection of 'bookmarks' in your browser software, to lead you to your favourite sites. There is nothing wrong with this, provided you don't prescribe that everyone must have the same collection of favourites as you. For scripture to retain its ability to respond to a huge range of situations, it is important that it not be narrowed down to suit the ends of sectional interests. There are a plethora of 'camps' within Christianity, each promulgating their own variety of dogma. Each of them holds some valid perspective or other, but distorts scripture by what is excluded.

If God is to be allowed to be God, and the Bible allowed to be the Bible, it will need to be set free from sectional interests. This includes denominational colonialism of scriptural territory. There is no need to raise flags and claim lands in the vast expanse of the Bible; there is enough to go round for everyone. The attempt to control people through manipulating access to scripture is a lost cause, and those who attempt to do so end up with their fingers burned every time. The Spirit breathes, blazes and dances through the Word, resisting confinement. This is cause for rejoicing rather than fear, celebration rather than control. Jesus assures us that the Spirit will lead us to truth, and the truth will make us free.

Moving On

This first section of the book has been concerned with what the Bible is and what it is not. There has been an attempt to provide some critique of the way in which scripture languishes in our culture, as well as suggesting a more positive analogy for understanding the way in which it works. All of this, however, is a little abstract. It is important to know not only what the Bible is, but also how it may be used to lead us closer to the heart of God. All sorts of descriptions are possible of a car; but in the end, most people will want to get in it and experience the sensation of driving. The rest of this book takes up that challenge.

Between Consenting Partners

People sometimes speak of an experience in which the Bible 'came to life' for them. I suspect what they mean by this is that it was the first time in which the text of scripture became a means of encounter for them with the living God. To use Martin Buber's categories, the relationship changed from 'I-it' to 'I-thou'. Or to return to the analogy of God's home page, for the very first time they logged on and established a connection. In so doing, the Bible was transformed from a dusty collection of historical trivia to a spiritual Tardis, capable of transporting the soul into the zone where God is waiting for us all.

My wife and I were baptized as adults in the Groynes. This was not a strange practice, but a place on the outskirts of Christchurch where there was a large pool of cold, clear water. Certain scripture verses had been selected for each of us by the group who were doing the baptizing. As we each in turn came up out of the water, these verses were read to us as a kind of gift. In my wife's case, the verse was 2 Corinthians 5:17, 'So if anyone is in Christ, there is a new creation; everything old has passed away; see, everything has become new!' What made this declaration hilarious was that as the words 'everything old has passed away' were read out, my wife's tattered sandal broke free from her foot and began floating jauntily into the distance.

In that moment there was a coincidence of text and event which broke the universe open for us, and had us laughing uncontrollably. Of course, it might have been coincidence. But the event had the unmistakable scent of the Holy Spirit about it, and it seemed a way in which God was adding the divine blessing to a special occasion. God has a hunger to be known, and responds to the frailest invitation by showing up in one way or another. So it is that the Bible frequently becomes a vehicle of encounter. The history of the people of God is a history of encounter, in which God initiates meetings. The Bible is a dangerous book, because it threatens constantly to breach personal boundaries and leave us exposed before God.

Engagement

Faith is never individualistic, but always personal. Which is to say that it is difficult to participate in the communal movement of God's people without having a personal engagement with God. At some level or other, scripture has to come to life for you and for me, in order that it can be vital for us. I wonder if it is not at this personal level that most Christians have struggled with the Bible in recent times. The private reading of scripture continues to be dutifully performed, but there is only so far duty can take you before weariness sets in. Unless such reading becomes a place of encounter, it is not likely to progress far beyond a routine and dissatisfying experience.

The problem lies largely in misapprehensions about the nature of scripture, as outlined in chapter 1. To treat the Bible as a book means that regular readings of it grow as exciting as reading a cookbook for the eighty-sixth time. We tend to come at it with the perceptual skills employed for tackling other bound copies of printed material, and that is where we come unstuck. Familiarity brings tedium, and we find ourselves completing the task of reading without having any of it register in any significant way. It is a digression from our everyday world into a gloomy museum which seems comforting only in its irrelevance. The words are present to us, but the Word remains silent.

In all this, it is well to remember that the Bible is a meeting place. It serves little if we turn up there on our own, do a little touring of the back streets, and leave without hearing anything other than the echo of our own footsteps. In personal devotional reading, the cry of our heart is to meet God, to walk a way in partnership and to return with our hearts burning within us. We want to engage with the Spirit, to feel the fire raging in our bones. I suspect this is what God wants too. But we too often come in the wrong way, like lovers turning up to dinner wearing a Walkman and headphones.

When engagement with God is our hope, then the heart is the way. We must learn to open our hearts, our imaginations, our psyches to the embrace of the Word. Sitting back passively and allowing our eyes to scan words is not the best way to do it. The life of prayer and the love of scripture are not two different disciplines in the journey of faith. They are one and the same. Both are ways of becoming receptive to God, to dropping the defensive mechanisms of a lifetime and waiting in complete vulnerability for our Lover to come to us. Both benefit from discipline, attentiveness and humility. To read the Bible in openness to God is to prayerfully seek engagement with the Word.

Deep reading

Reading scripture, then, needs to move beyond the superficial registration of words on a page. It is a reading at depth, a reading by the heart, a reading for encounter. People have different ways of encouraging this. To speak of techniques is to run the risk of cheapening the whole experience, as sex manuals can do to passion. But I offer the following illustrative examples as pointers along the way. They are hints rather than methods, and their purpose is to suggest the sort of reorientation that is required for the deep reading of the Bible.

Daydream believing

Ignatius of Loyola is credited with a way of approaching scripture which employs the imagination rather than the mind. He invites us to enter into the events of the Bible, rather than standing outside as spectators. It is a form of active wakeful dreaming, drawing on the same faculty which our dream life employs. Through engaging imagination in the conversation with scripture, the heart is opened to the presence and voice of God. It needs to be said that this way of reading is not applicable to every part of the Bible. It lends itself particularly to story segments such as the Gospels. Thankfully there is a great deal of narrative within scripture which may be brought to life through Ignatian reading.

Perhaps the best way to illustrate the approach is through example.

Let us take the passage Mark 5:24–34, in which a woman is healed of chronic menstrual bleeding.

> *And a large crowd followed him and pressed in on him. Now there was a woman who had been suffering from haemorrhages for twelve years. She had endured much under many physicians, and had spent all that she had; and she was no better, but rather grew worse. She had heard about Jesus, and came up behind him in the crowd and touched his cloak, for she said, 'If I but touch his clothes, I will be made well.' Immediately her haemorrhage stopped; and she felt in her body that she was healed of her disease.*

> *Immediately aware that power had gone forth from him, Jesus turned about in the crowd and said, 'Who touched my clothes?' And his disciples said to him, 'You see the crowd pressing in on you; how can you say, "Who touched me?"' He looked all around to see who had done it. But the woman, knowing what had happened to her, fell down before him, and told him the whole truth. He said to her, 'Daughter, your faith has made you well; go in peace, and be healed of your disease.'*

I come to this passage in an attitude of prayer, asking that God may lead me in my understanding. My initial task is to pick one of the characters in the story, and to adopt that persona through my imagination. It could be a member of the crowd, it might be Jesus himself. On this occasion I take the easy option, and choose the woman at the centre of events. I read the story through slowly several times, trying to feel my way into it. Then I employ my senses in the attempt to enter the story and become part of it.

> *I hear the babble of the crowd as we jostle for position. I smell the air of Palestine, with its faint odour of donkey mixed with stale sweat. Above me the sky is clear and blue, the sun blazing in a hot white glare. I feel the pushing and shoving as we compete to get closer to Jesus the prophet. I am too far back. It's hard for a woman to make a way through the crowd. Everyone wants to be at the front, and I'm not strong enough to push people aside. I can see him ahead, talking to people on either*

side as he walks. Close enough to see, but not near enough to touch. The story of my life.

I feel the despair settle on me like a warm blanket. It was stupid to come here anyway. I'm reduced to desperation now, chasing after phantasms. Who would have thought it would come to this? I had money once, and respect. I had my health. I believed in God and attended the synagogue, and it was all so easy. And then the bleeding started. Funny how women speak of it as the 'curse' when it only comes once a month. Mine was a proper curse; a perpetual bleeding that never stopped. My lifeblood seeping away, draining the strength and energy from my bones. As if that weren't enough, I became an outcast. I was unclean, for as long as the blood was flowing. Which meant always.

I don't blame my husband for leaving me. He couldn't come near me without violating his faith. He waited until he couldn't wait any longer, and I didn't hate him when he went. What else could he have done? There was the long round of consulting doctors. Every one with a different explanation and a different cure. Every one of them charging, so that my money oozed away as fast as the blood. Until I had nothing. Nothing and no one. Nowhere to turn. No hope of healing. If I was any braver I would have killed myself long ago, and put an end to it. But no, I keep on torturing myself with hope. And so I'm here, chasing after this miracle-worker from Nazareth. Not really believing but desperate.

A child falls in front of me and I step over him, lunging sharply into the press of bodies ahead. It catches them by surprise and I stumble into a gap. Without warning he's there in front of me. And now I scurry along behind, terrified. I shouldn't be here at all. Every time I touch one of these men I make them unclean. If they knew, if someone recognized me, who knows what might happen? Here I am with what I wanted right in front of me, but suddenly I'm too scared to ask. If I call out to him, they'll all stop and see me. I'll betray myself. And what if it doesn't work? I'll make a fool of him and myself. I've been to faith-healers before and it's never done me any good.

But there's a chance, a tiny chance. A crumb of hope that I can't ignore. If I just reach out, if I just touch his robe, if he's who they say he is, if, if, if... As my fingers make contact it's as if I've reached my hand into a cold stream. It fills the whole of me with calm, a deep wonderful stillness where my heart seems to be beating into a vast void. There is a burning in my loins as if there were fire on the inside.

And I can feel it stop. Feel the ebbing cease, the trickle stem. My body drawing itself into line, adjusting, becoming quiet like my soul. It's as if everything in the entire universe has stopped and is silent.

Except for that voice ringing out from the beginning of time. 'Who touched me?' They laugh, and I assume they're laughing at me. But it's him they're ridiculing. I try to press back into the crowd, but there's a wall behind me. I feel more naked than when I'm undressed; totally exposed and vulnerable. It's what I dreaded. I wanted to stay anonymous. I hoped to stay as I was in my familiar life and reach out and touch, but not to be drawn in. It was healing I was looking for, not involvement. To have things made better, not to emerge from the shadows and sidelines. But he knows already. And I know he knows.

I drop to my knees in front of him, crying out in terror. I want to explain what I've done, but it comes out as gibberish. I try to tell of my twelve years of misery, to describe my desperation, to ask forgiveness; but it all becomes a sodden muddle. And with his eyes he hears it all, and answers. 'Daughter, your faith has made you well; go in peace, and be healed of your disease.' Once again I'm in that empty space, where there is only the two of us and his voice. And now the burning is coursing through my whole being, cleansing and purging and sealing. The cocoon tears, he is gone, the crowd parts around me, I am on my own and on my knees.

My life has been given back to me. Except not just the life I had. A new life, bubbling and surging within me like a freshwater spring. All the dusty dead bitter parts of me have been sweetened and saturated and enlivened. The future stretches out before me like the path. I wanted to stay hidden, but I couldn't. And I

know now that to stay healed I must step out of the shadows
and into the light. I must walk and follow and speak and heal.
I have been made whole.

And now I begin to draw back from the story, and inhabit my own life again. It takes a few moments to make the transition. The scene fades, but I find the feelings linger. When I reached out to touch Jesus, something happened, both then and now. The peace and the joy remain. I linger for a time, thinking about my own tendency to hide and the places I do it. It seems to me that God has been calling me out of my shyness and rectitude; assuring me that it is safe to reach out and touch, that there is nothing to fear. This is the Word that stays with me throughout the day.

Meditations and mantras

Meditation has a sort of New Agey ring to it. And yet we find encouragement in scripture to meditate on the self-communication of God (see especially Psalm 119). For many years, I was never sure what to make of these sorts of injunctions. Only gradually did I learn that there was a way of savouring scripture which by-passed more conventional analytical or systematic approaches. It is what a colleague of mine calls the 'lozenge effect'. That is to say, instead of biting off great chunks of scripture and taxing our mental digestive systems, it is possible to take a small mouth-sized morsel and suck on it for a long time.

It can be a good thing to take a phrase or two from the Bible, and dwell upon the material for an extended period. Words such as 'There is therefore now no condemnation' (Romans 8:1), or 'Neither do I condemn you' (John 8:11); there are innumerable suitable portions. A helpful way to make them the subject of meditation is to employ them in a similar way to that in which mantras are used by the exponents of transcendental meditation. Which is to say, repeat the fragment of scripture over and over until it picks up a certain rhythm of its own and begins to sink down into the depths of the psyche. Ideally it should be possible to continue repeating it without conscious effort, though this may take some practice.

The aim is not to try to understand the scripture. It is not to draw out the meaning or use it as the basis of a sermon. Rather it is to engage with a small section of the Bible at a completely different level from that of our conscious analytical mind. Surprising things may result. After a period of time, the scripture begins to resonate with certain parts of our hearts, and eventually becomes an organic addition to our personalities. People who have never truly felt forgiven, even though intellectually sure that they are, may discover for the first time the gentle strains of mercy. Long-held resentments may begin to dissolve in the cleansing bath of love. The scripture that is the object of meditation refuses to stay at arm's length, and instead becomes inwardly active.

The art of retelling

Fortunately, the Bible encourages the art of retelling. The stories found there show the effects of generations of reshaping and reworking. Having four Gospels, each with their own slant on the life, death and resurrection of Jesus, is an affirmation of variety and the value of different perspectives. The apostle Paul was a great missionary because of his ability to take what was basically a Jewish story and tell it in such a way that it riveted the Gentile world. The Bible is never quite fixed, even though the canon is closed. It lives and breathes and takes on new forms to meet new eras.

Wherever in the world the church has gone, it has been involved in the task of Bible translation. The motivation here is to make the words of scripture accessible to people whatever their language or culture, so that they can access it and interpret it for themselves. The direction of movement is part of the incarnational initiative adopted by God; away from the source of revelation and toward the recipient of it. On the day of Pentecost we are told that everyone heard the proclamation in their own language (Acts 2:6). Translation is a form of retelling the story in a new context, in order that it may be understood and responded to.

Today's world is divided not only into cultures, but also subcultures. Among groups who share the same history, language and geographical location there can be wide diversity in tribal identity. Perhaps related to this there has come the growth of 'paraphrase'-type translations of scripture, which attempt to freshen up the language of the Bible in order to make it more accessible. One of the most successful of these has been Eugene Peterson's *The Message*. His facility with language has given new insight into familiar passages:

*Are you tired? Worn out? Burned out on religion? Come to
me. Get away with me and you'll recover your life. I'll show
you how to take a real rest. Walk with me and work with
me—watch how I do it. Learn the unforced rhythms of grace.
I won't lay anything heavy or ill-fitting on you. Keep company
with me, and you'll learn to live freely and lightly.*
(Matthew 11:28–30)

All of which is by way of providing encouragement to take up the
challenge of retelling for yourself. Those who've been on the journey
for a time sometimes find themselves mired by their very familiarity
with the words of the Bible. It is possible for that which is close to
become distant simply because of its proximity. We read but we do
not hear. We see but we do not register. We become casual handlers
of mysteries, losing the wonder amidst dutiful repetition. One
response to this is to translate passages of scripture for ourselves. Not
only to attempt the revitalisation of the language, but to locate
the events within our own local horizons. Again, an illustration may
illuminate.

How might we retell the story of the rich man and Lazarus, from
Luke 16:19–31? Here's my translation:

*In the middle of the city there was an apartment block. And in the
penthouse of that block there lived a successful businessman, who had
made his fortune on the stock market. He wore Armani suits, drove a
BMW, and ate out at the most exclusive restaurants every evening.
The front door of the apartments opened directly onto the street.
Security was tight, and the whole entrance was monitored by video
surveillance. Each morning, the same tired old homeless man would
perch himself next to the door, and set up his begging station. His
name was Lazarus. He had a form of skin cancer caused by AIDS. Of
course he should have been treated in hospital, but he had no medical
insurance. And so his open sores wept.*

*Lazarus was hungry. He learned where the garbage from the apart-
ments was put out, and often he would go rummaging through it to
find scraps of haute cuisine. Each day he watched the businessman
come and go, and each day the businessman tried to avert his eyes
from the pathetic specimen of humanity who littered his entrance. He
found the presence of Lazarus disturbing. Why couldn't these people*

take care of themselves, and make a decent fist of life? Several times he called security and had them remove Lazarus, but the old man always managed to find his way back. One particularly cold winter day, Lazarus died at his station. The businessman saw his rigid corpse with its sores and pustules, and it was all he could do to refrain from vomiting.

Lazarus was met by angels wearing Doc Martens, and escorted into heaven, where he found many of the street people he'd known on earth. As it happened, the very next day, the businessman choked on a chicken bone and died. He found himself in a dark place, where there was always more to be done and not enough time to do it. It was like a nightmare he couldn't escape from. And he sweltered in the rank humidity, constantly sweating in the furnace-like bowels of whatever institution it was that he served. One day he caught sight of a video monitor, on which he saw that filthy beggar dressed in Levis and drinking wine with Janis Joplin. He found the number, and gave Janis a bell to try to set up lunch. 'And while you're at it,' he suggested, 'you might like to send that old derelict over to me with a bottle of chilled Perrier to quench my thirst.'

Janis laughed. 'Man,' she said, 'remember that good life you had, and they way you used to walk past old Lazarus here every day while he was suffering? Yeah, well the thing is, things are different here. The boot's on the other foot. And anyway, even if Lazarus and I were to take pity on you, there's no way from where you are to where we are, or vice versa.'

The businessman was rattled. If only he could find his PA. 'There's one thing you could do for me, then,' he pleaded with Janis. 'Send Lazarus back to my club, and warn my friends there of what might happen to them if they don't change the way they live.' Janis said to him, 'They have Dylan and Cohen and U2; they could try listening to them.'

The business man looked puzzled. 'Who?' he asked. 'Look, if someone like Lazarus returned to them from the dead, they'd maybe listen to him.'

She replied, 'If they don't listen to the voices crying in their own streets, then they won't change the way they live even if someone rises from the dead.' And at that the phone connection dropped out, and the man was left alone.

I tell you this story because I lived in the same apartment building as the businessman. On the ground floor, you understand, and nowhere near as wealthy. I felt compassion for Lazarus when I passed him, and sometimes I would toss a few coins into his cup. But then I went on my way. I think he was an immigrant. I think he was from somewhere in the Third World. He never said anything; he just watched as we walked past. And since he has died, he haunts me in my dreams.

This is one retelling of one story. There are hundreds of other ways of doing it, limited only by the bounds of imagination. Of course the story changes somewhat in the retelling, and may even make different points from the original. But in the concentration, the delving behind the text for its message, and in the probing of our own contexts for resonance, we may find again that sense of encounter and transformation which indicates the brooding of the Spirit over the Word.

Speaking out

This suggestion is very simple. It stems from acknowledgment that much of scripture arose in oral form, and had its genesis in liturgy or story passed on verbally from generation to generation. Scripture was mostly spoken word to begin with. It is a different experience to listen to words and the vibrations they make in the air, than to use your eyes to decipher symbols on a page. Reading involves the mind and, sometimes, the imagination. I have found it helpful to involve the body as well, so that as much as possible of me is attentive to scripture.

And so when I read the Bible for my own personal devotional ends, I read it out loud. I both speak the words, and hear them spoken. This is not so easy to do on the bus, but most people can find a private place where it is possible to read aloud without aspersions of mental illness. It is difficult to explain what a profound difference it makes to access scripture in this way; the best recommendation is to try it for yourself.

Praying along

Scripture can be both an aid to prayer and a means of praying. Whatever mood greets you in the morning, there is sure to be a psalm which gives voice to your feelings. Even if it be a muffled depression or a barely suppressed rage, there are words from the psalmist to match your feelings. Sometimes we can neither find nor trust our own words to be able to give expression to the heavings of our souls. As Paul notes, there are occasions when 'we do not know how to pray as we ought' (Romans 8:26). At such times it may be helpful to take the words of scripture on our lips and make of them our prayer. There have been times when I have used these words from 2 Corinthians as a means of affirming hope in the midst of angst:

> ... *for we were so utterly, unbearably crushed that we despaired of life itself. Indeed, we felt that we had received the sentence of death so that we would not rely on ourselves but on God who raises the dead. He who rescued us from so deadly a peril will continue to rescue us; on him we have set our hope that he will rescue us again.* (2 Corinthians 1:8–10)

Scripture can also be used to inform and direct our praying. That is, we can read the words and allow them to draw us into prayer. We might begin with the beatitudes, for example: 'Blessed are the poor in spirit, for theirs is the kingdom of heaven' (Matthew 5:3). Our prayer in response might be something like this: 'Who, God, are the poor in spirit around me? I pray for Emma, who is broken and disillusioned after her miscarriage. I pray for Peter, still grieving over his redundancy. I pray for Brian, who is feeling discouraged by another rejection notice. And I pray for those who are poor not only in spirit, but in goods. For the homeless, the unemployed, the street people. May I make some tangible difference to them. May I be a sign of hope, a sign of the kingdom. And help me to recognize the poverty in my own spirit; my own nakedness and blindness and destitution. I bring all of that to you.'

There are so many ways in which to encounter God through the Bible. It is as alive and varied as is God. On our own, in the presence of the Spirit, between consenting partners; there we discover again the dangerous encounter.

#8

Hearing Together

Individualism has ripped the guts out of the Western church. 'Doing church' as an assembly of discrete Christian believers can feel like trying to build a tower with glass marbles. You end up frustrated, with nothing but a dangerous mess on the floor. Or to come at it with another analogy, attempting to worship in gatherings of Westerners can be as difficult as teaching harmonies to those born deaf. They simply cannot hear. Faith, while always generated in personal encounter, finds its natural expression in community. Taken out of this context, it becomes a bizarre parody of itself.

Perhaps the most dramatic representation of this is where the elements of communion have been tidied up in the interests of hygiene. From a celebration which began around the dinner table, with bread and wine shared by friends under the shadow of death, we have arrived at a stylized and sterilized ceremony. To find a communion table bearing individual thimbles of diluted grape juice and tiny precise cubes of white bread, or carefully manufactured cardboard-like discs, is about a big a distortion as it is possible to make without crossing the line of blasphemy. I recount this not in criticism of any particular church stream, but in sorrow at the common predicament of the Western church.

The tragedy is not in the neatly atomized ingredients of the Lord's Supper, but in the disparate and disconnected lives of the worshippers who consume them. When worship is the only point of commonality among believers, rather than the climactic expression of an under-girding common life, then it becomes perfunctory and misleading. Christian journey was always intended as a corporate adventure, not a heroic individual pursuit. It seems that the individualism generated by the Enlightenment has succeeded in accomplishing what the soldiers around the cross could not bring themselves to do: dividing the seamless cloak of Jesus.

Some of the trouble, then, that people have with relating to scripture may be due to the distorted context in which they are encountering it. When it is packaged as a book, it's not surprising that it is treated like one. Naturally enough, people consider book-reading a private undertaking to be practised in undisturbed solitude. But the Bible is not a book. It is a ground of encounter, and one which reveals its hidden depths only when restored to its rightful place in the midst of the community of faith.

Scripture and community

I think it was Juan Carlos Ortíz, the South American evangelist, who told the story of getting up to preach to his large congregation. His message was very short and extremely simple. 'Love one another,' he quoted from John 13:34. Then he sat down again. The worship leaders were rather surprised, but managed to get the show back on the road with some more singing. The next Sunday he got up to preach, and repeated the same words: 'Love one another.' Again he resumed his seat. This continued for a number of Sundays. Eventually his elders took him aside, and questioned why he was repeating the same text over and over. 'Well,' he replied, 'when the people start doing it, I'll stop preaching it.'

Scripture and community are so closely related that it is impossible to attack one without damaging the other. Their relationship is a chicken-and-egg one, resistant to prioritizing. Historically, Catholics have emphasized community and Protestants scripture, but such polarizing is unhelpful and unsustainable. The two reinforce and encourage each other. The Bible does not have a life independent of the community of faith, any more than the church can be true to itself without reflection on scripture. It is a case of co-dependency, in the best possible sense of the word.

The communal
character of scripture

The Bible is organically related to the faith community in a number of ways, and only really makes sense when that link is maintained.

Generated by community

If the Bible is a collection of bits and pieces, it is a collection generated by the community of people who have responded to God down through the ages. Many of the stories are the stories told around the fire at night, to remind the tribes who they are and where they have come from. The Exodus story, for example, tells the people that they used to be slaves until God heard their cry and set them free. The bits of liturgy found in Psalms and other places are fragments of the worshipping life of the community. The narratives describe what happened to the people at different times and in different circumstances. Even the letters of Paul represent the communal interaction of groups of believers scattered across the Empire.

The biblical prophets had communities of followers who travelled with them and recorded their words. And the words which they bring are words addressed primarily to the people as a whole. Much of the narrative thread of the Bible is the story of assembled groups of people. The law is simply the written record of the covenant between God and the community of Israel. The injunctions and regulations are intended to demonstrate how people might live as faithful members of that community. In all these ways, the material which has been gathered together in scripture is the product of living communities; groups of people sharing a tribal existence in which God is at the centre.

Preserved by community

Clearly there would be no such thing as scripture if it were not for an historical community of people who have faithfully preserved it. Even though we respect the Bible by allowing it to stand over the church and shape it, we acknowledge that it was the church itself which selected, collated and passed on the words which we find in it. From the careful retelling of stories to the painstaking copying of manuscripts by monks, it has always been the case that the community of faith has carried the words of scripture in its womb and kept them alive. And although frequently guilty of being over-zealous in its enthusiasm, it is the church which has fought against the corruption of scripture.

This is the type of conservatism which is valuable. By preserving the integrity of scripture, the church has kept alive the dangerous and subversive memory of the God who creates it. Even at the times when its institutional life threatens to choke out its spiritual life, the community has regress to the life-giving tradition faithfully passed on by earlier generations. Thus the very act of preservation is also the source of perpetual reform; a conservatism which fuels revolution. In this, community and institution are sometimes at odds, but the living word of the Bible continues to freshen and revitalize the people of God.

Birthed in community

It is in community that the Bible reverts to its deep purpose; that of shaping and steering the band of pilgrims in their ongoing journey. So often the Word of God is declared in the midst of the people. In such a setting it attains a majesty and clarity which may be lacking in quiet individual reading. You can sit in the privacy of your lounge and watch the video version of a film. But it is a different experience than that of being in a crowded theatre with the same events played out on the big screen. To listen to a recording on a Walkman is enjoyable; but it is not to be compared with dancing in front of the stage at a live performance. In the same way, scripture has its natural home in the congregation of the faithful.

In recent years the vehicle of communal proclamation of scripture has been that of preaching. I will have some more to say about preaching in the following chapter. In the meantime, it is enough to say that there are many other ways of encountering the Bible as a community, some of which will be surveyed shortly. As a generalization, it is true that the deeper the community life of a congregation, the deeper the sense of common journey, the closer the relationships and the more intense the shared experiences, the more profound will be the resounding of the Bible among the people. In such a context, scripture leaps from community of genesis to community of reception like a high-voltage arc bearing the sizzling creative energy of God.

The Bible is not simply generated by community, however. It also acts to create community among its hearers. It is the spoken Word of God which calls into being both the community of creation and the human community (Genesis 1:1—2:25). The very word for church, *ekklesia*, means those who have been 'called out' by God. It seems that wherever God acts or speaks, living communities spring forth like trees following the path of a river.

> *When the poor and needy seek water,*
> *and there is none,*
> *and their tongue is parched with thirst,*
> *I the Lord will answer them,*
> *I the God of Israel will not forsake them.*
> *I will open rivers on the bare heights,*
> *and fountains in the midst of the valleys;*
> *I will make the wilderness a pool of water,*
> *and the dry land springs of water.*
> *I will put in the wilderness the cedar,*
> *the acacia, the myrtle, and the olive;*
> *I will set in the desert the cypress,*
> *the plane and the pine together...* (Isaiah 41:17–19)

When the people gather before Moses after his trek up Mount Sinai, or before Ezra after rebuilding the temple, or before Peter after the experience of Pentecost, it is the word of God which is constitutive of their subsequent community. Hearing scripture together reminds us who we are as humans, and what it is that God requires of us. And the very least that God asks of us is that we learn to live together, love one another, and take responsibility for each other. We discover that 'those who do not love a brother or sister whom they have seen, cannot love God whom they have not seen' (1 John 4:20). Many Christians would prefer to take themselves off into a corner with God and pursue holiness undistracted by the complexity of personal relationships. But the Bible will have none of it. It provokes us into community.

Strengthening community

Paul speaks much of the 'body of Christ'. This phrase has inspired many a sermon, in which it is held up as a central analogy of what the church should be. However, I suspect that for Paul it was much more than an analogy. It was an essential reality. The body of Christ is a sign of the new order; an organic reality which marks a significant change in the way in which humanity relates to God. We might think we are responding to Christ as individuals, but in fact we are being incorporated into a new mode of existence, 'baptized into one body' (1 Corinthians 12:13) in such a way that we become 'the body of Christ and individually members of it' (1 Corinthians 12:27). Our primary locus of existence is no longer the 'me' of individual experience, but the 'us' of communal participation in Christ.

So much for the theory. The bulk of Paul's correspondence bears witness to what happens when the ideal is sullied by everyday church life. His missives testify to the infighting, tyranny, envy, prejudice, pettiness and moral failure in those early congregations. There is something about group process which brings to the surface all that is worst in people. Perhaps that is why it is so necessary to have scripture in that setting, recalling the people of God to the best that is within them. The Bible reforms and recreates the community, whenever it is proclaimed there. It feeds and strengthens the bonds of love which are so essential to communal existence.

As God's chosen ones, holy and beloved, clothe yourselves with compassion, kindness, humility, meekness, and patience. Bear with one another, and, if anyone has a complaint against another, forgive each other; just as the Lord has forgiven you, so you also must forgive. Above all, clothe yourselves with love, which binds everything together in perfect harmony. And let the peace of Christ rule in your hearts, to which indeed you were called in the one body. And be thankful. Let the word of Christ dwell in you richly; teach and admonish one another in all wisdom; and with gratitude in your hearts sing psalms, hymns and spiritual songs to God. (Colossians 3:12–16)

Confronting community

Communities, like individuals, are capable of wandering off track; of deceiving themselves and their members. Throughout history, the people of God have often lost their way or deliberately rejected it. One of the central paradigms for this in the Bible is the wandering of Israel in the desert after their liberation from Egypt. It is a story of a people who are in almost constant rebellion, complaint, lethargy, fear, resentment and distraction. Time and again, they need to be confronted with where they have come from, where they are heading, and who it is who is with them on the journey. In the contemporary pilgrimage of the church, that function of confrontation is performed by the Bible.

We gather to hear again who we are as a people and how God has called us out of captivity. We find ourselves reminded of our destination, and the reality of a kingdom which is yet to come. We are challenged to examine the way we are living in the light of the true nature of our journey. Such confrontations are not always pleasant. We prefer our illusions that we are nice, generous and faithful people. But scripture exposes the veiled greed, hatred, selfishness, lust, violence and cruelty of our existence. Our attempts at playing church through religious performances are rudely interrupted by the plain speaking of the Bible, and we are summoned once more to make choices as to future direction. In this way God is continually recreating us as a people, and calling us on.

Hearing together

There is a huge range of ways in which a community can encounter scripture together. Unfortunately many of them have been neglected under the domination of the sermon. It seems that as the Bible has become more accessible to the individual reader, so it has grown less prominent in the corporate life of the church. That is a loss which needs to be remedied.

The public reading of scripture

There is too much comment on scripture and not enough hearing of it. In some ecclesiastical circles, there is hardly an uninterpreted word of scripture left. I have been dismayed in recent years at the paucity of Bible reading in the Evangelical churches of my home country. This is the movement which has claimed such strong allegiance to scripture that it seems something of a betrayal to find it so neglected in their services of worship. There is preaching, to be sure. There is explanation, exposition, illustration, analysis, description, erudition and rhetoric. But it is rare to find any remnant of the Bible itself, unless it be a few verses which form the basis for the following oratory. I am sure there are some congregations which have forgotten that there is anything preceding the letters of Paul.

The Bible, when read competently in the congregation of the faithful, is sufficient unto itself. To hear the text ringing and singing is to once again recognize its magnificence. Some conditions are necessary to aid the process. One is relative calm in which to be able to concentrate together on the words. Another is some encouragement within the shape of worship that the reading of scripture is a significant event, and not something to be skipped over lightly. The recent practice of people following the reading in their own Bibles is in my opinion, while well intentioned, a source of distraction and the triumph of individualism over community.

The most important single ingredient, undoubtedly, is a skilled reader. Here is one area of the church's life where democracy should not apply. Rostered scripture readers are the equivalent of rostering surgery among the general staff of a hospital. We degrade scripture every time it is mumbled, slurred, mispronounced, rushed or stuttered over. A great work of art requires respect and attention to its presentation, and the Bible is no different. A good and gifted reader can bring scripture to life and make it accessible to the whole congregation. Poor readers will draw attention only to themselves. Let the Bible speak again in the gathering of the faithful! We will all be enriched.

Multiple readers

A simple method of presenting the drama of scripture is, where appropriate, to use a number of readers voicing the parts of various participants, perhaps with one as a narrator. This recreates some of the vigour and tension of the original passage. It's not even necessary that it be a biblical story involving several characters, although of course that is the easiest type of material to work with it. For instance, a section of Romans (7:7—8:2) might be made more accessible by dividing it into two voices as follows:

> What then should we say? That the law is sin? By no means!
> Yet, if it had not been for the law, I would not have known
> sin. I would not have known what it is to covet if the law had
> not said, 'You shall not covet.'

But sin, seizing an opportunity in the commandment, produced in me all kinds of covetousness. Apart from the law sin lies dead.

I was once alive apart from the law, but when the commandment came, sin revived and I died, and the very commandment that promised life proved to be death to me.

For sin, seizing an opportunity in the commandment, deceived me and through it killed me.

So the law is holy, and the commandment is holy and just and good.

Did what is good, then, bring death to me? By no means!

It was sin, working death in me through what is good, in order that sin might be shown to be sin, and through the commandment might become sinful beyond measure.

For we know that the law is spiritual; but I am of the flesh, sold into slavery under sin. I do not understand my own actions. For I do not do what I want, but I do the very thing I hate.

Now if I do what I do not want, I agree that the law is good. But in fact it is no longer I that do it, but sin that dwells within me. For I know that nothing good dwells within me, that is, in my flesh.

I can will what is right, but I cannot do it. For I do not do the good I want, but the evil I do not want is what I do.

Now if I do what I do not want, it is no longer I that do it, but sin that dwells within me. So I find it to be a law that when I want to do good, evil lies close at hand.

For I delight in the law of God in my inmost self, but I see in my members another law at war with the law of

*my mind, making me captive to the law of sin that
dwells in my members.*

Wretched man that I am!

Who will rescue me from this body of death?

Thanks be to God through Jesus Christ our Lord!

*So then, with my mind I am a slave to the law of God, but
with my flesh I am a slave to the law of sin.*

There is therefore now no condemnation for those who are in
Christ Jesus.

*For the law of the Spirit of life in Christ Jesus has set you free
from the law of sin and of death.*

Only by trying this with two voices does it become apparent how
much easier this makes a complex passage to understand.

Dramatized text

There are some instances in which a passage of scripture may usefully
be acted out before a congregation. Caution is needed in this area,
however, if the result is not to be second-rate acting by young people
wearing tea-towels on their heads. There are other dramatized texts
which have already found their home in Christian worship, such as
baptism and communion. In these sacramental actions, the word
takes on flesh in a way which communicates mystery and meaning,
and which links the congregation with an ongoing history of witness.
Both baptism and communion take up and portray the central
themes of the Bible. When the word becomes enacted in this way, it
has deep resonance with those who participate.

There are many variations on traditional church practice which are
able to revitalize that which has become overly familiar. With the
baptism of those old enough to survive it, for example, taking the
ceremony outdoors to a river or the sea provides drama which is not
found inside the walls of a church. Communion also gains much by
being relocated. One of the more moving celebrations I participated

in was the one described at the start of chapter 6, amid the rubble of a recently demolished hospital ward. And the elements can be changed to contextualize the sacrament. Here in New Zealand I have experienced the eucharist with everything from meat pies and beer to pavlova and chardonnay. Perhaps the most authentic version of communion I witnessed was a full meal provided for local boarding house residents, with no religious language at all. It was a profound expression of Luke 14:12–14.

Various pilgrimages can become acted out recountings of scripture. The traditional one which still has much to offer is that of the stations of the cross. Here the sense of movement and pause, retracing the steps of Jesus toward the cross, involves and moves people in a way that simply reading the text can never do. When I was minister of an urban church in Auckland, we would take the stations of the cross outdoors during Easter. Strolling the streets with a cross and a slowly beating drum, we would observe the stations at appropriate local venues; the trial of Jesus outside the police station, the taking down of his body outside the funeral parlour. It somehow brought together the events of the gospel with the real world in which we lived and worked.

Liturgical use

There is no reason why the Bible cannot be used as a vehicle of worship for the congregation. This can take any number of forms, from the setting of sections of scripture in a responsive prayer, to the communal reading of a psalm. Often scripture is set to music and sung together. While this can be very meditative, caution is necessary. The music used must be robust enough to stand the weight of scripture, and bear repetition. Otherwise it can tend to trivialize that which it carries, and transform it into a sort of jingle which makes it impossible ever to read the verses again without nausea. The monastic community of Taizé has done a good job of showing how text and music can be successfully joined without violence to either.

In the alternative worship movement, there has been an important discovery for participants in the emerging culture. That is the projecting of scripture on to the wall as an aid to worship. When this is combined with other still or moving images, there can be a profound experience generated by the juxtaposition of text with picture. Dancing to scripture verses also provides a new way of processing them in worship. There is a saying often used within alternative worship: 'If you don't move your feet, you won't understand the words.' In this setting, other creative uses of scripture have been experimented with, such as the handing out of cards with a varied selection of scripture upon them. Imagination is the only limit in this environment.

Discussion

Although this approach to the communal digestion of scripture will be addressed more fully in chapter 10, it is important to acknowledge it in a preliminary way here. Group discussion of passages of the Bible allows for the active participation of those involved, and so actively builds community both through the process and the subject matter of the process. To be effective, it requires a certain degree of trust among group members, and a willingness to delve below the surface. Too often such Bible study groups become exercises of the intellect, in which the person with the biggest concordance has the most to say. The purpose of group study should not be so much to analyse scripture as to bring the life of the group under its searching gaze.

A friend tells the story of being in a Bible study group with a man who was expounding the wonder of the peace of Christ. He assured the group that a deep understanding of this meant that despite untoward events in life, equanimity could be maintained. Others were doubtful that serenity was always possible in urban existence, but this saint was dismissive of their lack of true spiritual understanding. It happened that another member of the group had to leave early, but came in rather flustered a few minutes later to report that he'd just backed into the man's car. It wasn't until a few minutes into his visible rage that the exponent of peace recognized the contradiction. With the help of the group, he later became able to laugh at himself.

There are many ways in which scripture can be accessed communally, and it is vital for the welfare and faithfulness of the church that it is attempted. For most congregations, their primary sense of encounter with the Bible is through preaching, and to that topic we now turn.

9

We Don't Want
No Sermonizing

Some years ago my wife was moved to tears by a sermon. The preacher, with admirable pastoral concern, noted this, and after the service he sought her out to offer counselling. I imagine he was secretly pleased that his message had generated such a deep emotional response. He was therefore a little taken aback when she explained that frustration rather than conviction had generated her tears. 'I feel as if I came looking for bread, and have been offered a stone,' she explained. Of course that was in the early days of our Christian pilgrimage, when we still hoped for something significant in a sermon. As the years went by we became resigned to accepting that this was probably an unrealistic expectation.

But even in making that statement with all its cynicism, there is something within me which wants to protest. How can it be that we have come to such a lamentable state in the proclamation of the gospel that it has become something to be endured rather than an occasion of liberation? The term 'sermonize' is synonymous with arrogant, interminable lecturing. In the words of Sydney Smith, 'Preaching has become a byword for a long and dull conversation of any kind; and whoever wishes to imply, in any piece of writing, the absence of everything agreeable and inviting, calls it a sermon.' Much responsibility for the low view of the Bible among Christians can be traced back to preachers who have managed to render it drear.

Complaints against preaching, particularly among participants in the emerging culture, are legion. In amplification of the points raised in the Introduction, the following criticisms may be made of preaching in general. Naturally they do not apply to all sermons or all preachers. But they cover a substantial middle ground.

Too long

Attention spans are shortening by the year. While this may be lamentable, and a sign of intellectual degeneracy, it remains a fact of life. A new generation is used to concise, colourful presentations which are able to convey the essence of that which is to be communicated in a brief format. This is the culture in which the gospel is to be communicated. In that context, a forty-five minute sermon is as out of place as a pith helmet, and probably less interesting. The only form of verbal communication left in society of comparable length is the lecture. Perhaps this has become the unfortunate model which has been adopted in the church. Not surprisingly, the response of the faithful is more often glazed eyes than changed hearts.

Too abstract

I am dismayed by the number of sermons which are essentially theoretical in nature and intent. They deal with 'principles', and seem to proceed on the basis that the purpose of the sermon is the illumination of the mind. While intellectual rigour should be a criterion of good preaching, it cannot be the substance of it without distorting the nature of humanity. It is part of the modernist and liberal fantasy that sin and evil can be addressed through education. Titillation of the mind serves as something of a distraction from the hard task of following Jesus. The Word of God can never be processed and analysed into neat categories; it is far too dangerous for that.

Too preachy

I hope it is not a tautology to describe preaching as preachy. In my understanding, good preaching should never be preachy. I understand the term to mean a rather arrogant postulating of a way of life or course of action for others, by one who neither participates in or feels compassion for those who are being advised. It is the equivalent of lecturing on military strategy by someone who had never experienced battle, and is doing so from the comfort of the lecture hall. The smug certainty which results is not helpful to those who know the terror and ambiguity of real engagement.

Too moralizing

Moralizing is a great temptation for preachers, and a great distortion of the gospel. Perhaps the majority of people outside the church have the impression that Christianity is about a rather ascetic code of moral behaviour. I have many times heard people remark that they are 'not good enough to be a Christian'. How have they arrived at such a lamentable understanding of what the faith is about? In many quarters moralism has become the new legalism. As Jesus amply demonstrates to the horror of religious people, the gospel of love is seemingly scandalous and immoral.

Too impersonal

Some of the worst advice I ever received in my theological education was to steer clear of using personal illustrations in my preaching. I would go so far as to say that any preacher who doesn't speak out of the crucible of his or her own experience is not worth listening to. Frederick Buechner in *Telling Secrets* complains of ministers he has listened to:

> There is precious little in most of their preaching to suggest that they have rejoiced and suffered with the rest of mankind. If they draw on their experience at all, it is usually for some little anecdote to illustrate a point or help make the pill go down but rarely if ever for an authentic, first-hand, flesh-and-blood account of what it is like to love Christ, say, or to feel spiritually bankrupt, or to get fed up with the whole religious enterprise.[8]

Too didactic

There is a real place for instruction within Christian life, but the sermon is not it. Study groups, lectures or Christian education seminars are the places for passing on the knowledge which is an integral part of faith. Preaching, in my understanding, is not primarily an educational experience, but one of encounter and transformation. The goal is not imparting of information but persuasion, as much as they can be separated. It is regrettable that many preachers emerge from their theological training having adopted lecturing as their model of communication, and reproduce it for their long-suffering congregations.

Too authoritarian

For better or worse, there is not much communication in today's world which is uni-directional. People like to be able to talk back; to ask questions, to seek clarification, to offer alternative points of view. Authority is no longer accepted as a corollary of office; it has been betrayed too many times to have inherent credibility. And while it might be argued that the sermon is a place for people to be quiet in deference to God speaking, this is rather too grand and presumptuous a construction on the task of preaching. Good preaching will have an internal authority which does not need overt protections.

Too boring

It is hard to think of anything that I would not rather be doing than listening to the majority of sermons. And that includes cleaning someone else's hair out of the plughole in the bath. The only other experience I can recall which induces a similar catatonic state to that of an average sermon is the speechmaking at school prize-giving ceremonies. It is an unspeakable tragedy that the Bible should attract guilt by association, and be commonly regarded as being as boring as many of its advocates. Bewilderment is the appropriate response to the transformation of one of the most engaging stories of all history into a generator of ennui. It is an achievement of some genius, if also one of deep betrayal.

Some pointers for preachers

This section will be mainly of value to those who are engaged in some form in the public proclamation of scripture. Although this is a limited sample of people, it is an enormously important group in terms of the influence they wield in shaping the popular perception of scripture. The following suggestions are somewhat subjective and fragmentary, but they are hopefully constructive pointers on a way forward. It needs to be said that for all my cynicism and mockery, I am an advocate of the role of preaching. However, if it does not improve in quality and authenticity, I fear it will rapidly become as anachronistic as family singing around the piano.

The place of scholarship

Despite my earlier critique of the historical-critical method and its legacy, perhaps I need to assert the value and importance of creative and disciplined scholarship on the part of preachers. Those who dare to expound the Bible in public had better make sure they know what they are dealing with. Preachers need a working knowledge of the history, nature and composition of scripture, just as an electrician needs to understand the workings of electricity. In both cases, ignorance is dangerous. If scholastic enthusiasts are bad for preaching, they are not nearly as bad as the uninformed who parade their own prejudices and woolly ideas as somehow being connected to the Bible.

Anyone who takes their task seriously will do as much training and preparation for it as possible, in order to be proficient. The raw material of preaching is scripture, and preachers need to know its length and breadth, its landscape and features, its boundaries and hinterlands. Nor it is enough (though it is certainly a help) to read the text over and over. Some basic understanding of the history of the Bible is necessary, to understand how various sections of it relate to the life of the communities which generated it. What is the significance of the two accounts of creation in the early chapters of Genesis, or the four perspectives offered on the life of Jesus by the Gospels? How did Messianic hope arise in Israel, and in what ways did Jesus fulfil it? Why was Jesus crucified? These are questions which require some intellectual application to resolve.

Another advantage of study is to avoid the pitfalls of proof-texting. A little reflection on the history of scripture is enough to reveal that the Bible contains the Word of God deeply enmeshed within the life of the communities which responded to it. The treasure is always contained in jars of clay (2 Corinthians 4:7) or, to be more precise, in cultural packaging. Sometimes the cultural accretion needs to be stripped away to get at the precious material. Only when this sort of exercise is undertaken is it possible to discover that the gospel means liberation for slaves, for women, or for marginalized groups. In the absence of such study, the mere quoting of the Bible out of context becomes a basis for promoting cultural bigotry.

That said, however, the majority of people engaged in preaching have the benefit of having undertaken several years of textual study before being unleashed on the church. The major problem for such people seems not to be lack of knowledge of the text, but rather the assumption that such understanding is sufficient in itself to produce good preaching. This is to confuse the starting point with the process. When someone phones for an electrician because of a faulty socket, they do not want a lecture on the properties of electrical current. And neither, in general, does a faithful member of the congregation with a difficult marriage want a lecture on the history of circumcision.

Exegesis, to use the technical term for the application of scholarship to the raw text of scripture, is necessary but not sufficient. As a teacher of mine used to say, exegesis has some similarity to underwear. It needs to be there, but it doesn't need to be displayed. If we were to look for a primary cause of the dullness of much contemporary preaching, it would only be necessary to open the average biblical commentary and try reading it for inspiration or relaxation. It is not riveting stuff. Nor is it intended to be. It is background information, important enough in its place, but rarely capable of the persuasive and challenging role assigned to preaching. I suspect too many preachers spend too much time reading commentaries. They then serve up the results of their investigation to the congregation, padded out perhaps with a few illustrations. It is the gastric equivalent of a suet pudding containing very few raisins.

The purpose of study is to keep the preacher honest and informed in her or his handling of the text. It is no substitute for preaching, and it is certainly not suitable content for a sermon. Exegetical investigation provides a reasonable starting point for an encounter with the text. The fact that some parishioners may encourage the rehearsal of biblical trivia in preaching is not necessarily an endorsement of homiletical erudition. It may be that such people are grateful primarily because cerebral gymnastics confine matters to relatively safe areas for all concerned. Responsible preaching which is in dialogue with the Bible will shred all protective garments in its bid for engagement.

The art of persuasion

Preaching is not about making the content of the Bible known. The competent reading of scripture can accomplish that. Nor is it intended to promulgate some new ideas about the shape of the church or the latest fashion in spiritual experience. The purpose of the sermon is to unleash the power of scripture in a way that leads to personal and corporate encounter with God. It would hardly be necessary apart from the sinful bent of human nature, which as Genesis 3:8–10 so vividly describes, leads us to hide from God for fear of discovery. A good part of preaching consists of finding ways around the carefully constructed defences of supposed followers.

The arena of encounter between humanity and God is almost always the heart, rather than the head. And so the aim of preaching is not education but persuasion. The subtext of every sermon is that of conversion—the conviction in hearers to change some aspect of the way they live. Persuasion includes the recognition of human freedom and individual responsibility. Nobody can legitimately force another person to change their viewpoint or lifestyle. All we can do is to invite them to do so as persuasively as possible. And it is this invitation which forms the core of the Christian Bible. The task of preaching is to create a space in which people can hear that invitation for themselves, and choose their response.

I used to tell theological students in the homiletics class, half jokingly, that a sermon is a sacrament of listening. The assembled people are listening for the Word of God. Because of this, sometimes they hear it, despite what the preacher has to say. As evidence for this, I suggested they analyse the messages which people will say they have got out of a sermon, when the preacher knows that nothing of the sort has been mentioned. It serves to keep sermon-makers humble. However, it does not excuse them from their responsibility to do the best job possible in persuading people to seek the kingdom of God.

The methods of persuasion are different from those of education. The former requires trust, understanding of the hearer, insight into common defences, compassion for difficulties of response, clarity of purpose, personal commitment to the cause, clear elucidation of the issues and the ability to engage the deepest feelings of the heart. Intelligent and articulate people make good lecturers; intuitive and self-aware people make good preachers. In contradiction of much Evangelical orthodoxy, I would contend that the purpose of preaching is not systematic exposition, but piercing encounter. In every good sermon there will be a moment of intense discomfort, during which the congregation will find themselves made vulnerable and aware of the presence of God.

If the preacher has had no personal encounter with the text, then there is nothing surer than that the congregation will not have one either. It is out of the preacher's own struggle to live the life of faith that preaching is born. Disengagement is the cardinal sin. It is easy for preachers to forget that their task involves exegeting the world with all the enthusiasm and dedication which they bring to exegeting the text. The call for those involved in sermon construction is to live homiletically; that is, with all the senses attuned for the meaning and significance of existence. The world is harder to exegete than the Bible. After all, the text is neatly provided; but the questions which must be brought to the text for the purposes of preaching can only be gleaned from participation in the culture.

Identity is the starting point. No one can preach incisively while remaining outside the context of the hearers. Surely this is part of the message of the incarnation: God entered fully into our human condition in order to speak in a way in which we were able to understand. Preachers must be participants in both their surrounding culture and in the human condition. They must hear and feel the questions and protests which are contained in the angst-ridden society that enfolds them. Altogether too many Christians are guilty of answering questions which no one else is answering. Too few have felt the full force of terror and dismay which unbelief stirs in the heart. And yet without this, preaching is taking place in a vacuum.

Some clergy live in a state of practical dualism, separating out their personal lives from their ecclesiastical responsibilities. They regard their own experiences of pain and isolation as weaknesses which must be concealed, while a brave front is presented to the congregation in order to encourage faith. This is to utterly short-change God, themselves and their congregations. It is only in the encounter of the text with personal experience that authentic preaching can flower. As Buechner laments,

> *Sad to say, the people who seem to lose touch with themselves and with God most conspicuously are of all things ministers… Ministers run the awful risk, in other words, of ceasing to be witnesses to the presence in their own lives—let alone in the lives of the people they are trying to minister to— of a living God who transcends everything they think they*

know and can say about him and is full of
extraordinary surprises.[9]

It is hardly convincing to speak of the light when you have never encountered the darkness. In the face of personal anguish, a preacher who gives the air of never having suffered or doubted can appear unbearably smug. The secret of preaching is that it is the word of God inextricably bound up and rooted in the human experience of the person proclaiming it. This is not something to be regretted but celebrated, because it opens the possibility that the same word might take root in our poor broken lives. If the preacher has seen something of what we have seen, has felt something of what we feel, has suffered something akin to our own pain, and can still preach the gospel; then there is genuine and substantial hope for us. That alone is almost enough to make us believe.

The common journey

A sermon is a common journey, and the preacher is the guide. All too often the preacher is fully equipped and eager to get under way. She or he can be tempted to stride off into the distance, not thinking for some time to flick a glance over the shoulder to see if anyone is following. Unfortunately, the assembled congregation is preoccupied not with some far-off destination, but with the immediacy of their own concerns. While they may wish to be followers of Christ, for the meantime they are weighed down with burdens of financial constraint, familial conflict, relationship difficulties, self-doubt, health concerns and secret fears. The first task of the guide is to gather everyone together and help them begin to move forward from where they are.

The first few minutes of a sermon, a story or a film are vitally important. If the people are not with you after this time, it is almost impossible to capture their attention again. In church, people often make good use of the sermon time to wander off on their own private reverie, not to be stirred again until music announces that this interval is over. Preachers have to work hard at the beginning, in order to enter into the world of their hearers, engage them, and lead them forward to begin the journey of encounter. It requires an incarnational movement; a willingness to enter into the world of the congregation to greet people there, rather than calling them from a distance.

A good guide will know the path to be travelled from personal experience, and will have a reasonable idea of the destination. Such a person will anticipate the travellers' fears and questions, and will walk beside them to provide encouragement at every stage of the journey. On any pilgrimage, there will be places of rest and places of exertion; times when the going is tough and requires concentration, and times when everyone can relax and coast for a while. It is the responsibility of the guide to be aware of and provide for such variation. The good preacher is ever alert to fellow travellers, discerning their mood and watching for stragglers. Even preaching is essentially a pastoral task.

In some ways the destination and route of the sermon is always different; in others it is always the same. The place of arrival is always that space in which God is present, and in which the text of scripture is enflamed by the Spirit and begins to do its work deep within the human heart. What happens here is beyond the preacher's control, just as healing is ultimately beyond a physician's control. All we can do is provide the conditions for it to take place. In the preacher's case, this requires leading the people to a place in the desert where there are no more excuses or compromises, and in which they stand exposed before the winds of divinity. Perhaps it needs to be said that it is important that the person doing the leading has been to this place before.

Nor is it enough to leave people stranded in the desert. They must rejoin the territory of common life which they know so well. A way back needs to be provided. Hopefully the returning flock will be transformed and inspired, their wills attuned toward that of God. But this is not the responsibility of the preacher. It is enough to provide guidance to the place of encounter and back again. What happens there is up to God and the effective power of scripture. Preaching is as much a mystery and a sacrament as is communion. The guide is only a companion on the way, albeit one who provides a sense of direction to the whole enterprise. They should not draw attention to themselves, but to the destination and the One who waits there.

Creative models of preaching

This is not a book on preaching, and there is no space for a comprehensive treatment of the subject. However, the dominance of expositional and deductive preaching in the contemporary church calls for some alternatives, lest the faithful continue to suffer unnecessarily.

An inductive approach

In simple terms, a deductive method begins from first principles, which are then enlarged and illustrated to apply to experience. By contrast the inductive approach is to begin with common experience, and through investigation of it arrive at some significant truth. When applied to preaching, the difference is in starting with the text (deductive) or starting with experience (inductive). Of course in some ways all preaching begins with the text, in that the preacher must engage with it and have some sort of encounter before the exercise can get under way. But when it comes to the proclamation of the text, both deductive and inductive methods of communication are legitimate.

I want to make a case for the inductive approach, after generations of deductive orthodoxy. I have several reasons for this. The first is that Jesus used it frequently. Analysis of the parables demonstrates that they begin in the world of common experience, where the people live their everyday lives. Jesus begins where the people are, and leads them to the living God. Secondly, in terms of the common journey of preaching, I have already made a case for the importance of the beginning. It is the responsibility of the preacher to enter the world of the hearers, and not vice versa. This is enabled through an inductive approach. And thirdly, the Bible has become increasingly estranged from the world of the faithful in recent times. This is due to the combined effect of scriptural neglect and a rapidly changing technological world, laden with ethical dilemmas. If believers are to come to the text, they need some help to be led there.

As an example, here's an introduction to a sermon I preached some years ago in response to John 21:1–14:

> *It's a well-known fact that on any given Sunday morning, fifty per cent of the congregation feel like they've been dragged through a gorse bush backwards and hung out to dry. This has nothing to do with what they did Saturday night. It has everything to do with feeling like the biggest fraud on God's earth. Here you are singing hymns, pretending to pray, working hard at looking interested in the sermon, and all the time keeping the lid on a mass of contradictions. Your heart is*

*not full of peace, your mouth is not full of praise, and neither
your hands nor anything else is lifted up. Jesus seems like a
remote and shadowy figure, and whether he died or rose again
is not nearly as important as if you turned the stove off or not
before you came. Mostly you come to church because you'd
feel too guilty not to, and because your friends are here.*

It is a long journey from here to the text, but it is an attempt to enter
into and engage with the real people who are present in the pews.
The inductive approach to preaching offers respect and assistance to
those struggling to find the Word of God in their ambiguous lives.

Storytelling

Preaching is a stylized form of storytelling, and many of the skills necessary to telling a good story are common to those of delivering a
good sermon. There is much scope for developing the narrative
nature of preaching. In these postmodern times, storytelling is perhaps the primary means of communicating matters of significance.
This becomes clear when we consider that films are simply visually
presented stories. The methods of the story are quite different from
those of a lecture, and yet it is the lecture which seems to inform the
majority of preaching. A return to the narrative roots of both scripture
and the historical tradition of Christian preaching may bear much
fruit.

Stories are complex, and operate on a number of levels. They do
not always move in a directly linear fashion, even though they
invariably involve progression. A story may not be immediately self-
revealing, but may leave the listener somewhat undecided and
needing to do further reflection and work. I think this is a good model
for sermons. I find much preaching simplistic and patronizing, in that
it presents me with pat answers and leaves little room for my own
contribution of searching and imagination. By contrast, the hidden
depths of a story may continue to work long after it has been told.

I am not speaking of the use of sermon illustrations. These short
narrative vignettes are helpful, and are often all that is remembered
from a sermon. Nevertheless, they are simply illustrations to aid the
digestion of an essentially deductive and cerebral form of communication. What I am arguing for is a new appreciation of the narrative

style in reconceiving the entire task of sermon making. As an example, I have delivered sermons that were nothing other than short stories. One, based around Ecclesiastes 1:5, 6, recounted the adventures of a man who received a magic chequebook through the mail. As much as he spent would be deposited in the account at the end of each month. But he had to learn to spend freely, and in accordance with the generosity afforded him. Stories are ambiguous, and some thought I was encouraging fraud. But there were others who made connections at a deep level.

Dialogue and interactive preaching

The apostle Paul uses an interesting technique in many of his epistles. He sets up an imaginary dialogue between himself and an opponent. One of the great benefits of this approach is that it opens up the topic by allowing a polarity of views, and allows the reader to fit themselves into each of the voices in turn. The same technique can be used to break open the mono-directional nature of sermons. It is most easily done with two people, who if they are able to spark off each other and enter into the spirit of it, can make the experience enjoyable as well as engaging. But it can be done with one person. One memorable example involved playing the part of a marital counsellor, responding to an imaginary visit by Joseph and a very pregnant Mary.

Sermons can be interactive in a number of ways. It is possible to react to questions or comments from the congregation, or to begin with a piece of music which raises existential questions. In the church where I was minister for many years, the sermon was invariably followed by a 'Free-for-All' time, in which response to the sermon was both allowed and encouraged. The freedom provided included arguing point-blank that the preacher was wrong or misguided. Many times the discussion which ensued was more memorable than the sermon, and certainly served to provoke further reflection and response to whatever text had been addressed. Such sessions were always chaired by someone other than the preacher, to make it easier for people to speak freely.

There is much more which could be said about preaching. Suffice it to say that the current state of affairs is lamentable, and in need of comprehensive reformation. The Bible is too good a resource to handle shabbily.

#10

Unleashing Scripture

For century after century, people have been speaking of the power of scripture to transform lives. At the same time, others whose lives are intimately connected to the Bible through calling or profession can be bewildered by such assertions. They read, proclaim and study scripture, but have never had any personal experience of the Bible as anything much more than a majestic book. How is it that the same resource can generate such different responses? I think the answer is that the Bible requires a little work to access its transformative qualities.

Defences and evasions

Many of us have elaborate and carefully constructed defence mechanisms, which we have developed for the sake of our own survival. The positive side of such defences is that they preserve us from danger and enable us to live in an aggressive world without fear. Unfortunately, they can also be used to protect us from change and growth, and lead to the premature relinquishment of the painful pursuit of life and truth. Psychoanalysts are well aware of the ploys which people engage in to avoid confrontation with unpleasant discoveries about their own personalities or behaviour. Such 'blocking' is a form of neurotic behaviour—an avoidance mechanism—and can be present in a highly sophisticated form among those who profess religious belief. After all, God is a pretty heavy dude to have knocking on your door!

In order to unleash the power of scripture, it is necessary to get on the inside of defences. So although the purpose of this chapter is to survey some ways of liberating the Bible within human hearts, it may be helpful to address some of the barriers which need to be circumvented.

Avoidance

The simplest way to evade encounter with scripture is to avoid it. And perhaps the most successful means of avoidance is to give the impression that it is central to your life. Some Christian people have developed interesting strategies on this basis. These include carrying around a large study Bible, memorizing verses of scripture to be quoted at every opportunity, stocking bookshelves with biblical commentaries and adorning walls with plaques bearing various King James platitudes. So it is not always obvious when a person is guilty of avoidance. The test is not proximity to scripture, but engagement with it. The most successful weeds grow close in to the stem of healthy plants.

Of course nowadays such unconsciously duplicitous behaviour is not so necessary. There seems to be decreasing expectation that Christian people will relate to the Bible, either in a superficial or a meaningful way. It is almost as if there is a growing culture of avoidance within the church. Certainly it is much easier and more comfortable to be a Christian without the words of Jesus ringing in your ears. So much of what he has to say cuts across the grain of contemporary existence, and only serves to complicate life. Much more pleasant to fashion a tender Jesus, who has some jolly good ideas, speaks kindly to children and dogs, and winks both at deep-pile carpet and foreign sports cars. After a while, it hardly seems necessary to have him up on the cross at all.

Distraction

In the words of Kurt Cobain, 'Here we are now, entertain us'.[10] We have become a generation cultured into distraction. There is always something able to be switched on which will draw and hold our attention while we 'blob'. From an armchair we can summon up services undreamed of by the wealthiest emperor of a few centuries past.

But as much as our reach is broad, so it seems to be correspondingly shallow. At a time when recreational pursuits are more available than ever before in history, there is also a corresponding rise in complaints of boredom. I suspect the reason for this is that many of the forms of entertainment we consume are passive and escapist. They require nothing of us other than our attention, and leave little with us other than the occupation of our time.

Pain- and reality-avoidance is an industry. We live in a world of euphemism, spin-doctoring, sedation and virtual reality. It is assumed that a life in which there were no death, suffering, loneliness, commitment or sacrifice would be a qualitatively better existence, and so we do what we can to build such an illusion. There is little appetite left for confrontation with self, others or God. From this point of view, the Bible is hopelessly out of date. It addresses unpleasant topics such as greed, lust, evil, betrayal; and asks of us discipleship, compassion, confession and repentance. It suggests that the choices we make in this life are of real consequence for our eternal destiny. No wonder we prefer our distractions. However, the tragedy is that they do not satisfy, for they are relatively insubstantial.

Justification

Those of us who have a reasonable knowledge of the Bible find ourselves in an invidious situation, in that we quickly run out of excuses. We know what is required of us, and we know how far short we fall. Scripture can be blunt in its demands. The only viable defence is that of justification, which is another term for twisting the meaning of scripture until it supports rather than challenges our compromises. We find a selection of verses that will support us in our unbiblical lifestyles, so that we can claim scriptural support for justifying ourselves. Sometimes we manage to convince ourselves; most of the time we are tragically aware of the hollowness of our attempts to fool God and others.

Perhaps the most obvious area in which this is true for Western Christians is that of materialism. One of the areas Jesus talks about most is that of wealth and possessions, and yet we are shameless consumers, no different from those who make no claims of faith. The ultimate in justification is prosperity doctrine, which teaches that wealth is a sign of God's blessing, and that the deeper your faith, the richer you will get. A pity Jesus didn't know about it. But at a level slightly below this blatant distortion of scripture, there are the commonplace justifications we make for our new houses, cars and furniture. All of which is a way of saying we know we shouldn't be living this way, but we don't seem to be able to help ourselves.

Disobedience

The stakes are raised a little when we come to this level of evasion. Here we are quite clear what it is that the Bible asks of us, and yet unwilling to conform. And so, effectively, we say 'no' to God. At the end of that exquisite section of Jesus' teaching called the Sermon on the Mount (Matthew 5:1—7:29), there is a chilling reminder that it is not enough to hear. Obedience is the true sign of belief; not mere affirmation. Firstly Jesus speaks of those who will try to gain entry to the kingdom of heaven on the basis of their miracles, but who are turned away with the words 'I never knew you' (Matthew 7:23). And then he goes on to explain more fully what he meant.

> *Everyone then who hears these words of mine and acts on them will be like a wise man who built his house on rock. The rain fell, the floods came, and the winds blew and beat on that house, but it did not fall, because it had been founded on rock. And everyone who hears these words of mine and does not act on them will be like a foolish man who built his house on sand. The rain fell, and the floods came, and the winds blew and beat against that house, and it fell—and great was its fall! (Matthew 7:24–27)*

In some respects it is better not to know. Once we have heard the words of Jesus, we gain a new responsibility for the way we live. He calls us not simply to believe, but to follow. Were it not for his abiding words of forgiveness, and his gracious and healing restoration of the disciples, many of us within the church would have real reason to fear the consequences of our disobedience. And even then, it may be a better course to turn around our lives than to presume too much upon grace.

Disbelief

Sometimes our failure is not so much one of direct rebellion as of failure of courage and imagination. In the face of a complex world, the kingdom of God seems too fragile and faint a vision to hold. We find ourselves swamped by practical demands, which are a lot more tangible than the apparently esoteric territory of the Bible. Consequently, although we may read and even preach from scripture, we regard it in a similar way to fairy stories; pleasant and interesting, but nothing to do with reality. Our lives become split between the real world in which we make decisions and build for the future, and the 'spiritual' realm which is regarded as something like the Twilight Zone, and equally insubstantial.

While failure of belief can be involuntary, it also becomes a convenient means of reducing the tension between the vision of the Bible and human life as it is experienced. By placing scripture into the category of impossible dreams, we effectively consign it to a place where it has no bearing on our practical living. Even the most dedicated of Christians experience something of this lapse in imagination when it comes to Jesus' kingdom teaching in the Sermon on the Mount. By elevating it beyond history, we make it impossibly utopian and so dismiss its claim on our own lives. This, like the others, is a form of evasion.

Antidotes and interventions

If we are to experience the force and majesty of scripture, it is clear that we will have to counter our own predilection for avoiding encounter with it. The following suggestions are intended to provide some mechanisms for doing just that.

People who know us

As has previously been argued, the Bible is written among communities for communities. It is in its natural element when among a group of people who have made a commitment to each other and to God. Many of the defences which we construct are viable only because they exist within the outer perimeter of our individual privacy. We are able to deceive ourselves because there is no one with the right of entry to challenge us. Our reading and interpretation of scripture is considered to be in the private domain, and therefore beyond scrutiny. It is little wonder that our innate human selfishness and penchant for self-justification lead us astray from time to time.

There is no substitute for a group of fellow travellers who know us thoroughly. In my early years of the Christian journey I considered myself to be a reasonably spiritual sort of chap. That was until I spent a year living in intentional Christian community with a group of others. We shared not only a house, but also incomes. The veneer of friendship did not last terribly long. A host of petty frustrations arose: the way someone folded the newspaper, inappropriate uses of the dishcloth, differences in philosophy of childcare. Once a week we met to discuss common issues. These sessions often became gruelling times in which we charted a course through personal conflict. The experience seemed to bring out the worst which was within each of us.

And yet there were unexpected benefits. From the base of our communal house we hosted a weekly group for prayer and Bible study. It became a venue in which it was very difficult to hide behind a false piety. As we approached scripture, it was in the full light of the shabbiness of motives and unreconstructed greed which might have been exposed earlier in the week. Because we had travelled the distance together, because we depended upon each other in our daily lives, because we knew each other, those of us in the house were able gently to strip away each other's defences and evasions. It was a painful process; but it was also a time of tremendous growth, as the Bible spoke to the deepest parts of us.

In an ideal world, a church might provide such a community of people in which we know and are known. The proclamation of scripture among us would then be of a different character. But unfortunately, many churches are of a size or nature which makes it almost impossible to develop relationships at depth. The most we can hope for is some small-group experience within the larger congregation. If such a group works hard at relationships and is willing to endure and grow through conflict, then the possibility emerges of accountability. That is another way of saying that people may begin to trust each other enough to earn the right to speak into each other's lives. In that setting our evasions begin to be revealed for what they are, and we find the confidence to step forward into the full glare of the Bible, accompanied by friends.

In tackling materialism, for example, there is no way in which this can be addressed by individuals. To live a lifestyle contrary to that of all around is psychologically very difficult for a person on their own. Resistance requires the power and support of a group, who are putting themselves on the line in solidarity. Only in a group can we begin to hear and respond to the searching words of Jesus on possessions and how they affect us. There needs to be a venue where fear and misgiving can be expressed, where anger and resentment can be expressed, and where prayer and forgiveness can be expressed. Scripture both depends upon and creates such community.

Engagement

Because the Bible comes to us in the form of a book, it is tempting to keep it at arm's length. We scan the words with our eyes, process them with our minds, and get on with life largely unaffected. This is to have the form of scripture without the power of scripture. It is an acquaintance with scripture without encounter; perusal without passion. Over an extended period of time, it becomes possible to develop low expectations of the Bible, and to be satisfied with too little. In such cases, it may be necessary to experience a form of shock treatment to the soul, in order to revive it from slumber. This can be done by the temporary circumvention of natural defences.

In an intriguing book called *Transforming Bible Study*,[11] Walter Wink presents a way of approaching scripture which does just that. He notes recent discoveries concerning the way we process input with the opposing hemispheres of our brains—the more rational approach of the left hemisphere contrasted with the feeling and intuitive work of the right hemisphere. His contention is that too much of our interaction with scripture has been dominated by left-brained approaches. While not in the least downplaying scholarship (he himself is an academic), Wink argues that there is a need to engage scripture with the more artistic, metaphorical and spiritual side of our natures.

In order that we may experience a transforming encounter with scripture, Wink advocates a method which gradually unfolds the depths of significance in a particular text. The setting is a group one, and the process requires a leader who has done considerable preparation. The major task of the leader is to ask a series of questions, and to refuse to provide answers to those questions even when pushed to do so. The threefold investigation of a particular part of the Bible then begins with the slow and meditative reading of it. The first questions are those of clarification and understanding. They help the group to dig down into the text and uncover its setting and purpose.

Secondly, the process moves to questions which Wink terms those of amplification. Here the method is similar to the Ignatian one described in an earlier chapter, inviting application of the imagination to the text, 'where we try to live into the narrative until it becomes vivid for us'. The third and most important stage is that of some exercise of application. This is where the rubber meets the road; where human spirit meets scriptural vitality in an often wrenching engagement. Right-brained techniques such as drawing, sculpting, music and small-group discussion are some of the means which are used to bypass defences. Wink reports that it is at this point that most resistance on the part of the group is encountered.

It is not possible to do this method justice in summary, but it is powerfully transformative. The following is an example of questions Wink suggests in confronting Mark 5:24–34 and its gospel parallels (provided to the group), the incident of the woman with the menstrual flow already treated in chapter 7.

• In Mark, when is she healed? When is she healed in Luke? In Matthew? If she was healed immediately upon touching Jesus, why does Matthew make it the consequence of Jesus' word to her? Why does Mark have verse 34b? (Compare NEB.) As the tradition develops, what is happening to the relative roles of the woman and Jesus?

• What is the woman suffering? What were the social consequences of her bleeding? How do you think she felt about her body?

• Why does she sneak up behind him in the crowd? What gives her the courage to touch him, if all other physicians have failed?

• How would you account for her healing? List the possible explanations.

• Why is the woman afraid (v. 33)? What has she done to Jesus by touching him? Why does Jesus make her own up to what she's done? What does this add to her healing? Why must it be public?

• What is 'faith' as depicted in this story? Define it on the basis of what is in this story alone.

• What is the role of Jesus in her healing, if it is her faith that healed her?

• Divide into pairs. For two minutes one of you say to the other, 'If

I touch his garment I shall be _____ ... If I touch his garment I shall be _____', giving a different statement of your need for healing each time. After one gives as many answers as possible within the two minutes, reverse roles. (The leader should announce when the two minutes are up. Afterwards give them some time to reflect with each other on what they heard themselves saying.)

Vulnerability

It is a difficult thing for all people, Christians included, to make themselves vulnerable. All our instincts are tuned for preservation, and vulnerability entails genuine risk. If we lay down our defences we are temporarily open to attack and consequent harm. And yet, in the approach to scripture as to God, vulnerability is the appropriate attitude. Deep in the centre of our tradition is the example of Jesus who 'though he was in the form of God', yet 'humbled himself and became obedient to the point of death—even death on a cross' (Philippians 2:5–8). For the sake of us all, Jesus relinquished such legitimate defences as were available to him, and submitted himself to the will of God.

There is an unpleasant strand of competitiveness which runs through Western Christianity; a sort of spiritual one-upmanship which forces people into defensive positions. In such an environment it becomes difficult to become open and honest, because of the awareness that others are always jockeying for superiority. Scott Peck speaks of the culture of 'rugged individualism' which suppresses our humanity:

> *It encourages us to hide our weaknesses and failures. It teaches us to be utterly ashamed of our limitations. It drives us to attempt to be superwomen and supermen not only in the eyes of others but also in our own. It pushes us day in and day out to look as if we 'had it all together,' as if we were without needs and in total control of our lives. It relentlessly demands that we keep up appearances. It also relentlessly isolates us from each other.*[12]

And, we might add, from God. It is this sort of emotional armour-plating which becomes a real barrier to the encounter with the Bible.

The solution, naturally enough, is to find ways of laying down our defences so that we can truly hear scripture. A few words of qualification are necessary. Vulnerability only makes sense in an atmosphere of trust. This is not such a problem in meeting with God, but can become one in the context of a group of people. It is sensible to seek a safe place in which to become vulnerable, where there is an expectation of confidentiality and compassion. And very importantly, vulnerability is something which must always be chosen, and never imposed. Even the expectation that others should open themselves is a form of manipulation. We are only responsible for our own level of risk-taking. Indeed for some people with deep hurts, vulnerability with others may be counter-productive to their healing.

That said, there is a need to undercut a great deal of the defensiveness which permeates Christian institutions, and which serves to insulate us from scripture. Somebody needs to start, and perhaps the place to begin is with leaders who are secure enough in themselves to practise a personal form of unilateral disarmament. They may teach more by example than by any number of sermons.

Contextualization

There is a very simple yet profound way of releasing the power of scripture among a community of people. It is to allow the Bible to speak into the context of the hearers. In general we manage to keep the revolutionary stream of the text within safe boundaries. We assume it has to do with church and ministry and evangelism and holiness. These are the issues which concern us in our 'religious' mode of being. Equally, it is generally assumed that the Bible is not particularly relevant to a different range of issues, such as who we vote for, what we do with our money, how we educate our children, where we invest our discretionary time, which programmes we watch on television or what drugs are acceptable to use.

The split of existence into the realms of religious and secular is dualism, and dualism is always dangerous to Christianity. The one God has created the one world, and life in God must remain seamless. In our century, many Christians in Latin America have experienced a genuine revolution through the simple strategy of reading scripture in the context of their poverty and oppression. The encounter between the Bible and their everyday lives has become explosive, since the time they stopped excluding sections of their existence in their approach to faith. They learned to bring the questions, contradictions and protests of life in the *barrios* (slums) to their reading of scripture, and the result has been one of radical transformation.

We in the West have much to learn from the hermeneutics of our South American sisters and brothers. It is time we began asking a few hard questions of our own in the presence of the Bible. Such as? Such as why the problem with society is always beneficiaries and never wealthy entrepreneurs. Such as why it is wrong to want to offer basic services such as health and housing to all members of the community. Such as why some of us can be strident in our opposition to the death penalty at the same time as accepting huge numbers of abortions. Such as who it is that controls the media and how perception is being shaped by it. Such as why there is not enough work to go around. Such as whether there is any connection between our own wealth and the comparative poverty of much of the rest of the world.

Questions which make us uncomfortable, but which also are enmeshed in the fabric of our existence. God is not the God of our private religious affairs, and neither is the Bible a collection of moral precepts to reassure us in our lives of comfortable consumption. Contextualization is simply a process of breaking down the artificial walls between faith and existence. It helps to locate our own struggles for practical love, justice and the pursuit of God within the horizon of an overarching movement within history. We have our own stories to live and our own Pharaohs to confront, and God continues to be interested and involved in the outcome. The Bible may not give us clear answers to our own issues, but it will provide a penetrating perspective.

Action

A book can be read and understood, and so fulfil the purpose for which it is written. Not so the Bible. The appropriate response to scripture is not an improvement in knowledge, but a change in lifestyle. For too long the Evangelical church in particular has tended to be satisfied with a shift in belief patterns as evidence of conversion. This would be fine if belief were regarded as more than a verbal affirmation. As Jesus clearly indicates in Matthew 21:28–31, his idea of obedience is one which is reflected in deeds rather than words. Where there has been a genuine encounter of an individual or a community with scripture, the result is change revealed in action.

The Bible can only be understood by those who are prepared to put it into action. As such, it must be regarded as a scientific theorem. It needs to be put to the test of experimentation in order for it to make much sense. The South American liberation theologians have described such an approach to faith and theology with the phrase 'action–reflection–action'. In other words, commitment to the cause of God is primary, and should lead to involvement in the world for the sake of the kingdom. Out of such practical involvement arise the questions which lead the activist back to scripture and reflection. And then, as a consequence of such reflection, changed and better informed action should ensue.

To use a rather trite phrase, 'Faith is a verb, not a noun'. Following Christ is impossible from a stationary position. It is necessary to get up, leave your place of belonging, and fall in behind Jesus. This inevitably means leaving some things behind and changing some modes of behaviour. The Bible makes no more sense to a sedentary reader than a map of Albania to someone who has never ventured beyond Chichester. It is not necessary to understand all or even much of the Bible; what is more important is that the little which is comprehended be translated into action. Subsequently, much which previously appeared obscure may become clear.

A story of conversion

In 1985 I became minister of a small and struggling congregation in central Auckland. In previous years, the church had contemplated closing down, and their confidence in the future limited them to offer me a job for the next year only. One of the things I did in that first year (inspired by the Church of the Saviour in Washington DC, a highly committed urban congregation), was to call together a small group of young adults who wanted to deepen their faith. We called the group 'Mission Group', for want of a better name. From the outset I made two things clear: that membership of the group entailed a high level of commitment to the other members, and that our common discoveries would eventually find an outworking in some form of practical service in our community.

For the first period, we did nothing much but study the Gospels and get to know each other. We kept a journal of our meetings and discoveries. At first it was reasonably superficial stuff. But as the trust levels grew, we became more honest with one another and the scripture we were studying began to stir us at deeper levels. We were aware of a gradual transformation of ourselves and our aspirations. After some two years of living with the Bible in the context of our group, we ventured out into the community. We decided to run sports evenings for disaffected youth. Hardly any came. Those who did come were psychiatric patients from nearby boarding-houses. Gradually it dawned on us that these were the people that God was sending us.

From the base of that dozen or so people, there unfolded an extensive ministry to the surrounding psychiatric community. The sports evenings were supplemented by film evenings, outings and all-in feasts. A concern for the accommodation needs of our new-found friends led to the formation of a housing trust, named the Community of Refuge Trust. It rapidly purchased some twenty-four units of housing, including a huge community house where psychiatric patients and nominally 'well' people shared their lives together. Today it has an asset base of some $2 million, all of it at the service of the people who occupy the housing. There grew interest in housing issues, and involvement in political campaigns. Ponsonby Baptist Church became a point of acceptance and a sign of hope for many of the local marginalized people.

All of this from a group of people who met together to read the Bible once a week. The power of scripture should not be under-estimated. To those who both open it and stand open before it, the Bible unleashes the power of God.

11

A Load of Old Flannel

When our three children were quite young, we read a book which spoke of the importance of 'family devotions'. As good Evangelicals, we were convicted about the lack of any effort in this direction, and decided to institute something immediately. We went off to a Christian bookshop, and purchased some suitable material, which from memory consisted of a daily scripture reading followed by comprehension questions geared toward children. The breakfast table seemed the most appropriate venue for such education to begin. I spent some time preparing for the first occasion, and we were looking forward to the time when our family would truly be a 'Christian' family.

And so we started. The first problem was the Bible reading. It may have been just a tad too long, and the translation may have rendered it a little obscure for toddlers. At any rate, the children became restless after the first few sentences and the reading had to pause to call them to attention. I'm not sure who poked whom under the table a few seconds later. Who started it was less important than the fact that within a few moments, a low-level skirmish was under way. Furrowed brows and meaningful looks meeting a wall of indifference, I was again forced to interrupt the reading to call for order. By the time we got to the questions, mayhem was erupting. I suspect I swore at the children; certainly I shouted at them, and produced the response of stony silent sulking. That was our final attempt at family devotions.

Children are wonderful, gorgeous, frustrating, spontaneous, infuriating, disarming, attention-seeking, innocent, cruel, entertaining, demanding and charming. Despite all the qualifications, they remain a gift of God to the human community. Christian parents naturally enough have a desire to do all that they can to nurture faith within their children. Churches have a responsibility to offer support, growth and encouragement to the children in their congregations. An important part of this involves helping children to develop a relationship with the Bible which will serve them in their journey toward adulthood. Unfortunately there is a great deal of confusion abroad regarding the best way of doing this.

My own children are grown up and finding their own way in life now. It is some years since I have had to face up to any practical responsibilities in communicating faith to children. So the following reflections are made by someone who is a bit of an observer and a non-participant. I would not dare to make them at all, were it not for the heartfelt cries I hear from desperate parents and providers of children's programmes.

Some things to
know about children

Children aren't adults

While observation should have removed any profundity from this revelation, the way in which children are treated in many Christian settings makes it worth repeating. In the worst of situations, church services are conducted as if there were no children present, and the unreasonable expectation is made that younger members of the congregation should endure in silence an experience designed entirely for adults. Children have different ways of processing things, different attention spans, different learning methods and respond to different stimuli from adults. A simple but not entirely satisfactory solution to those struggling with how to include children is to design the entire service around children. Many adults can find more engagement in these than in their normal fare. But the more sensible approach is to recognize that there are both adults and children present, and make provision for both.

Children think concretely

It is not until later in the developmental period that humans gain the ability to think in the abstract. Because adults have learned to think abstractly, and because they are usually responsible for designing children's learning experiences, they can easily fall into the trap of offering material and events for younger people which are basically incomprehensible to them. 'God' is a highly abstract notion. It is much easier for children to cope with Jesus or the prophets or even the concrete proposition of an old man in heaven with a white beard than it is for them to have any realistic notion of a divine being. And when it comes to scripture, they will not be nearly so interested in principles or lessons as they are in events and details.

Children learn differently

The ancient wisdom of Confucius (now a cornerstone of community development)—I hear, I forget; I see, I remember; I do, I understand —is particularly relevant to children. It is no good telling children a bunch of stuff and hoping that they might learn through the experience. To greatly over-simplify matters, they learn through a combination of observation and experimentation. They constantly need to try things out for themselves, to put new possibilities into practice, if they are going to make it a part of their ongoing learning. To encourage this, they need permission, encouragement and safe environments. And they need adult friends who are capable of thinking like children.

Children like to play

One of the great gifts of childhood is the ability to play, and one of the tragic losses among some adults is that they somehow grow out of that ability. Play is fun, self-motivating and enabled by the engagement of the imagination. As has hopefully already become apparent, the imagination is one of the primary vehicles of perception in approaching scripture, and its fostering and encouragement in the early years will build a good basis for the future. Good parents and teachers have known instinctively that play is a great incentive for and aid to the learning process for children.

Children like to ask questions

I have been driven to distraction by the questioning of my children at various stages of their development. There comes a time of particular frustration when young children learn the value of the single word 'why?' It becomes a useful means of extending the length of conversations, particularly near bed-time. Not all questions asked by children are serious. When a four-year-old asks where babies come from, it would be silly to offer a detailed description of human biology. While 'from the stork' is not an ideal answer, it probably addresses the question more on the level at which it is asked. Mixed in among all the endless interrogation of children, however, there are serious questions essential to learning. The task of the parent or teacher is to discern which they are. Important theological questions invariably arise at odd times, such in the midst of cleaning the toilet. Fortunately they don't require erudite theological answers, but they do demand an appropriate and encouraging response.

Children are not always nice

Over-romanticizing children is just as much a mistake as its opposite. Although there are aspects of children which undeniably are adorable, there are other traits which are just as saddening. Children can be selfish, cruel, competitive, wilful, destructive and exhausting. The issues which they face are ones which are appropriate to their level of development, but they do have temptations, transgressions and the need for forgiveness and restoration. There is much in the Bible which can help them attain a healthy balance in their physical, emotional, social and spiritual growth. As has been emphasized here constantly, the Bible is an aid and accompaniment to relationship with God, and that relationship is as rewarding for children as for adults.

The Bible and families

What happens in the home is of more importance for children than what happens at church. Particularly in the early stages of development, the home environment is massively important for growth. Relationships and attitudes here will have far greater impact than those experienced anywhere else. So it is at this base level that an orientation toward scripture will be forged.

When it comes to families, there are no 'norms'. The home context will be influenced by a variety of factors, including culture, income and personal history of the adult/s present. There are many ways of achieving the same tasks, and over human history many variants have arisen, particularly in regard to parenting. It is silly to come up with one pattern and prescribe it as the 'correct' way. Different settings will involve unique ways of providing encouragement, admonishment and humour. In every family setting, therefore, an approach to scripture needs to be harmonious with the particular environment in which it is found. There are some general principles which are useful, but the final shaping of them must be left to those who have responsibility. For me and my family, the whole idea of 'family devotions' was something which was destined for abject failure. It was an inappropriate cultural imposition, a form of behaviour which works in some settings, but is no more universally appropriate than a particular breakfast cereal.

And while we're on the subject, it is perhaps important to say that there are no guarantees with children and faith. I well remember a respected minister who hosted a group of young parents in his home for supper. Later on he took us into his study, and proudly showed us photographs of his children, who were now adults. He reminded us of Proverbs 22:6, 'Train children in the right way, and when old, they will not stray.' This was the promise he had counted on with his own offspring, he told us. Unfortunately, within a year, one of his sons who had been training for ministry had gone completely off the rails. His marriage was ended and he was drinking heavily. The fact is that parenting is a sharing of the experience of God; we offer what we can in love and guidance, but eventually our children must be free to find their own way through life.

Do what I say, not what I do

Children learn primarily by observation. The most important thing in forming attitudes to scripture around the home will be the attitude which parents exhibit toward the Bible. If it is loved, used and appreciated, then children will gain a positive orientation toward scripture which may last them a lifetime. On the other hand, if it is neglected or ignored, no amount of formal reading of it will suffice to convince children of its significance. The single most important thing which a parent can do to shape a child's regard for the Bible is to respect, value and use it within their own life. It is sadly not enough to put up a few selected scriptures on the wall. My son, who was learning to read, was impressed with a plaque bearing such a section of the Bible at a friend's place. He was sure that it read: 'As for me and my horse, we will serve the Lord.'

Story, story, story

Children love stories. They thrive on them, absorb them and always want more. Not only is the Bible full of stories, but there are many talented writers and illustrators who have managed to present such stories in words and pictures which engage and excite children. There is simply no substitute for the bed-time reading of such stories, in which the child becomes an active participant, looking at the pictures and asking questions. It is a place of trust and settling, one of the most intimate times between parent and child, and the perfect place for introduction of scripture in a digestible form. The ensuing discussion may lead off at any number of tangents, and is a vital part of demonstrating to children that the stories of the Bible have connections with what happens in the lives of people today.

Game-playing

It is relatively easy to take advantage of children's natural love for playing games so as to build their relationship with scripture. If I had young children now, I would be on the hunt for good imaginative computer games which introduced them to the world of the Bible. I would be thinking about how to combine play with learning. I think I would have words from simple verses cut up on fridge magnets, so that each week children could try to arrange them in the right order to make sense. I would keep my eyes open for any board games which might be helpful without being corny. Games are accessible, fun and potentially important learning aids.

Festivals

Christian festivals are opportunities for learning. There is much to be learned from the Jewish Passover tradition of getting the children to ask questions in order to prompt the retelling of the tradition. The secret here is that the learning experience doesn't start with words or ideas, but with an event of some kind. The explanation comes in order to make sense out of the activity which is being participated in. This is the right way round to do things with children. Instead of the mindless buying of chocolate Easter eggs, why not make and bake hot cross buns with the participation of some young assistants? There is something of a tradition in this part of the world of collecting a monarch butterfly cocoon around Easter time, and keeping it until the butterfly emerges. It provides a great means of talking about resurrection. When our children were young, every Christmas morning we would all join with the church in distributing gifts of food, cigarettes and money to local boarding-house residents. And that before the children were allowed to open the majority of their own presents! It was something of a highlight of the year for them, and gave them an appreciation of the true meaning of Christmas which persists still.

Owning their own

As early as practical, it is good to give children their own copy of the scriptures. There are some marvellous children's Bibles around these days, with superb pictures in them. For children, participation is everything, and the knowledge that they are entrusted with their own Bible can be very significant for them. At this stage of life, growth is rapid, and it may be necessary to change the version which they have at frequent intervals. Access to scripture in a form catering for them helps to stimulate the imagination and give children a sense of inclusion and regard for scripture.

The Bible and church

My early days with the church date back to the era of flannel-boards, promise-boxes and signs in church invoking silence and reverence. For those who are mystified by some of these elements, it is best not to ask. Suffice it to say that for many years in the history of the church, children have been considered a necessary evil. No attempt was made to accommodate anyone within the service who did not have adult cognitive ability. In Matthew 19:13–15, we find the disciples seeking to prevent people bringing their children to Jesus for a blessing, and being told off for doing so. Jesus welcomes the children, 'for it is to such as these that the kingdom of heaven belongs' (v. 14). It is therefore a sad state of affairs if children feel unwelcome in the midst of the worshipping community.

It is difficult to separate use of the Bible in a congregation from the general atmosphere toward children which prevails. Children are very good at picking up the emotional atmosphere in an environment, and knowing when they are wanted. The best children's programme in the world will not make much headway among a group who see young ones as a nuisance. As a result, the following suggestions are as much to do with the general church environment as the specific relationship of the Bible to children.

Acceptance and inclusion

One of the fundamental aspects of the Christian gospel is that of belonging. The presence of Jesus makes a space of acceptance for many who would normally be excluded on a number of grounds. This applies to children. To feel unwelcome or marginalized in a church service is a contradiction of the essence of the gospel. In the end, the nurture of children within a congregation will be dependent not so much on good teachers or brilliant programmes, but on the attitude of the members of the congregation toward children. Like the disciples, we adults are often keen to keep children out of the road and away from Jesus. This is because we have a high opinion of our own status and importance, and a lesser one of the concerns of children. Jesus seems to view things differently.

Children make noise. They cry out and run around and bang things loudly. Many adults find this a distraction, particularly when they are trying to listen for some pearls of wisdom from the front, or wanting to relate to God in quiet contemplation. As a minister, I have listened over many years to the complaints of people on opposing sides of the divide: parents who get nothing from a service because they are intent on keeping their children distracted and quiet; and adults who get nothing from a service because they are distracted by the noise of children. The answer has always seemed reasonably simple to me. There are different needs present which deserve respect and attention, within an over-arching responsibility to assure everyone that they belong and have a part.

As a generalization, I would say that church services err on the side of being too much oriented toward adults. They are highly verbal and cerebral, the sermons go on too long, and there is an unrealistic expectation of calm and quiet throughout the entire service. While there need to be times when children and their parents are expected to exercise restraint and responsibility, there are other times when children should be free to be exuberant participants. I have found that when there is space and place provided for children, they are much more willing to offer a corresponding allowance for the needs of adults. Children are the heritage of every member of the congregation—not just the parents—and should know themselves loved, welcomed and encouraged by all the adults present.

Involvement

It is not hard for any stream of church tradition to find an appropriate way for children to be involved in participating in the worship service. Whether it be handing out notice sheets, taking up the offering, lighting candles, praying or reading the Bible (selectively), children value and appreciate having a role to play. They are, after all, members of the community, with their own special gifts to contribute. A church which is friendly towards children will constantly be looking at ways of promoting their involvement, and making them feel welcome. If there is a separate children's time such as Sunday School, it will help to display artwork and other products of the children's creativity for the whole community. It can be a mutually rich experience to link older members of the congregation with children, so that they develop a particular bond.

Messy stuff

Most churches run some sort of educational programme where the attempt is made to present the Bible to children at an accessible level. There are all sorts of materials available these days for groups with enough money to pay for them. Some of it is good. A lot of it is not. The most common problem (whether represented by the material or the teacher) is the attempt to convey too much of a 'message' and to make sure that children have got it. I would not be particularly concerned with this at all, particularly with younger children. In fact, I would not be anxious if they came out with a quite mistaken idea of what a particular passage is about, as long as they had interacted on some level with a section of scripture, and were aware that that was where it had come from.

The best way for children to get involved with a text is to get their hands dirty. In this respect, many of the traditional Sunday School methods have been right on track. The elements of exegetical appreciation for children are paint, crayons, playdough, glue, paper, scissors, clay, glitter, cardboard, water, fabric and anything else that can aid the imagination in the creation of stuff. After the competent retelling of a biblical story and some discussion of it, the best strategy is to allow children to interpret some element in the way they see it, and give them whatever materials are necessary for it. In fact, this is the same technique used in spiritual direction with adults, often to profound effects. For children, it just comes naturally.

Drama

Children love to act, and adults mostly love to see them do it. One of the highlights of the church year for one of the churches I was associated with was the Christmas play. We were fortunate in having a highly creative congregation, so that what could have been a stodgy routine was invariably transformed into an experience of surprise and delight. The basic strategy employed was to write as many parts as necessary to include all children and all age groups. The scripts were always entertaining, often funny, and sometimes questionable in their interpretation of events. But everyone had a good time, and over a period of years the children naturally got to know the Christmas story thoroughly.

Public performance is not necessary, however, to the use of drama as an aid to learning scripture. Setting a group of children free to read, discuss and enact a section of the Bible is a brilliant way to get them familiar with and excited by the stories contained there. The combination of body movement and imagination is the perfect way for them to learn at their developmental stage. Allowing them to play with either the plot or the characters is not detrimental to scripture, but a means of them being able to bridge between the biblical and contemporary worlds. And of course the Bible is a treasure trove of suitable material, full of dynamic scenes and engaging characters.

Ritual

Ritual is a stylized form of drama, in which the entire congregation acts out the central stories of the Christian faith. We have already rehearsed the importance of ritual as a means of biblical appreciation. It is worth noting that where children are allowed access to such celebratory events, they become significant for them as well. For this reason, I think it is good for children to be able to receive communion. They don't understand the theological nuances of the eucharist, but they do recognize it as being something significant for the congregation. And they will simply receive it at their own level of comprehension, even if it is only as food and drink. It is probably better that they experience this central drama as one of inclusion than one of exclusion.

Pilgrimages of any kind can be wonderful learning opportunities for children. We should never underestimate the power of such simple events as following a cross along the street at Easter time. Our annual procession at Ponsonby Baptist Church always involved children taking turns at beating the bass drum, and usually there was a child helping to carry the cross. The re-enactment provided a way to retell the story for our children, and for them to identify as members of a witnessing group. When we stopped along the way to read passages of scripture, they were given context and meaning by the sense of journey. The event invariably provoked strings of questions afterwards. The text of the Bible was not something from the distant past, but an acted out reality on the familiar streets of our community.

Growing up with the Bible

Part of recognizing that humans are developmental creatures is a recognition that our ways of responding to the outside world change as we get older. Our means of processing sensory input, categorizing it and responding to it are variable according to stages of maturity. This applies to every area of life, including faith development and relationship to scripture. Children can only be expected to have a child's understanding of the Bible, and adults need to come to scripture as adults. In recent times, the church has done reasonably well in addressing these two ends of the developmental progression. But we have not done so well in assisting and supporting the transitional phases which lie in between.

Children's questioning comes in the context of a trusting relationship with adults, and with a broad acceptance of authority structures. But the questioning of adolescents is more searching and demanding. There has tended to be a rather large drop-out rate among late adolescents, particularly among those who undertake tertiary education. I suspect that a large part of this is because there is little scope given for young people to do their exploration of and questioning of scripture without a heavy-handed reaction from the guardians of the faith. There is little understanding of the need for adolescents to reject the foundations of their authority figures, in order to find a place for themselves. In some settings they are expected and encouraged to maintain an attitude of child-like trust when it has become entirely inappropriate.

As Jesus understands in his post-resurrection encounter with Thomas (John 20:24–29), serious questioning and doubting is not necessarily antithetical to faith, but may be the evidence of its presence. Teenagers become cynical because it is their duty to do so. We need not be afraid of their seeming lack of reverence. The Bible does not need people to protect it from attack. It has been resilient now for quite some time against the most searching of examinations. What adolescents require most is safe space in which to pull the universe apart, and adults who will stick with them despite testing and provocation. If they are to carry faith with them into adulthood, it will need to be a faith which has stood up to rigorous examination. I suspect the most helpful role the congregation can play in the process is to give permission, encouragement and stability through this process.

The gospel of Luke recounts the intriguing story of Jesus at the age of twelve wandering off from his parents (Luke 2:41–51). In many ways it is a paradigm of the adolescent journey. Although Jesus begins the journey with his parents, during the course of it he separates from them. They don't know where to find him; there is some anxiety that he has been lost to them. Anyone who has been the parent of teenagers will be familiar with this experience. When they eventually locate him, Jesus is asking questions of the teachers in the temple. This is entirely appropriate. His parent's questions and answers are not sufficient for him; he must ask and investigate for himself. He has his own journey to undertake, and his own learning to do. He needs to take responsibility for finding the way; all adolescents do. We must learn, like the parents of Jesus, to set our children free.

Nor is it only at the adolescent transition where the Bible needs revisiting. At various stages in people's lives, there may be external events or internal upheavals which create a revolution in the soul. At such times Christian pilgrims need nurture, encouragement and freedom as they reorient themselves in relation to scripture. There may be a whole new set of questions generated and brought to the encounter with the Bible. It is vitally important that the church not only allow but also support such times of growth and transition. The Bible is a resource for the entire journey, not simply the beginning of it. Used with wisdom, it both assists and lures us to grow up into God.

#12

Art for Art's Sake

There was a time when the church was known for its patronage and support of the arts. Churches were repositories for many of the great works of Western art, and some of the most sublime music ever created was intended for the church. Artists were at home in and valued by the ecclesial institution. That era seems long gone now. In some ways it was a part of the extended reign of Christendom, and came to an end with the demise of that period of Christian supremacy. However, it seems that the pendulum has swung too far in the other direction. A few centuries of Enlightenment rationalism have left the church a drab and prosaic shell. Those post-Reformation churches which I visited while living in Switzerland, stripped bare of anything vaguely resembling an image, are testaments to the broader iconoclasm of the entire Christian movement.

Never, I suspect, has there been an age more receptive to the artistic expression of spiritual themes than the one we inhabit. The advent of postmodernism and its renewed appreciation of holism (the understanding that all things are interrelated and belong to a greater whole) provide an environment in which art thrives. I firmly believe that if the church is to find a way ahead in this context, then it will not be by the application of systematic thinking. It is time for us to look to our artists to provide stepping stones in the broad river which separates the church from contemporary culture. Unfortunately, years of neglect and undervaluing of their work have left many artists disenchanted with the church. Extending a renewed welcome and restoring appreciation of their role will be a long-term project, including the revisiting of a theology of art.

An important part of this process will be the fresh encounter of artists with the Bible. The emerging culture has hardly begun to interact with scripture, and by and large remains isolated from it. Even from the perspective of art history, any self-respecting artist will understand the centrality of the Christian scriptures in the West. Now that the cultural authority of the Bible has been shattered, there exists the wonderful opportunity for a new generation of artists to begin a highly creative and unprecedented dialogue with scripture. The church has a role to play in promoting such dialogue, but it will need to understand the extent and limits of its role if disaster is to be avoided.

Towards a theology of art

Particularly within the Evangelical movement, the place of art has often been misunderstood as a covert evangelistic tool. This has resulted in two consequences; the fostering of bad art (that which is a thinly veiled carrier of 'message') by the Christian community, and the corresponding marginalizing of responsible art (that which arises out of genuine artistic vision). Our aim is the encouragement of artistic dialogue with the Bible. But in order to allow for this, we need to do some theological reflection on the nature of art.

Enjoyment

It's possible for Christians to become entirely too pragmatic and functional. Sometimes we dismiss anything which is not serving any immediately apparent purpose. Art, in theological interpretation, is simply the human participation in the divine love of creating. And if we look to that paramount description of God's creativity in Genesis, we discover an interesting qualification. In Genesis 1:1—2:4, the passage is shot through with a particular phrase which follows each creative act: 'And God saw that it was good.' In fact, when the entire creative symphony is over, there is a great deal of divine satisfaction: 'God saw everything that he had made, and indeed, it was very good' (1:31).

In other words, God enjoys what has been created. It brings pleasure in and of itself. As yet, none of the human drama has begun to unfold. There is no purpose evident or sought in these early stages. The results of creation are good in and of themselves. God takes pleasure in them. Creation and beauty need no other justification than their simple existence. Somehow, a sense of guilt seems to have attached itself to the Christian appreciation of aesthetics, as if it was morally wrong to enjoy that which is beautiful without qualification. The essence of art lies in both the creative act which produces it, and the appreciation of that which has been produced. Beauty needs no justifications other than itself. The enjoyment of it is a sure sign of the reflection of God's image within humanity.

Creativity

At the onset of creation, the Bible pictures the spirit/wind/breath of God hovering over the chaotic depths. This is as good a picture of the creative endeavour as we could hope to get. Later on in Exodus, the first person in scripture to be filled with the Spirit is Bezalel, so that he might possess 'ability, intelligence, and knowledge in every kind of craft, to devise artistic designs, to work in gold, silver, and bronze, in cutting stones for setting, and in carving wood' (Exodus 31:3–5). In other words, he has been divinely inspired to be an artist. Indeed, his list of talents makes him sound like a gypsy street-trader. Creativity, the soul of art, is the gift of God for the edification of the community. The Bible is full of artistic expression, with music, dance, poetry, liturgy and drama helping to celebrate and respond to the goodness and grace of God.

To be human is to be creative, and in being creative we find our fullest expression of humanity. To some among us, as with Bezalel, there is given unique gifting in order that they might enrich us all with their artistic ability. All of us find ourselves strangely moved by great music or painting. The vision of a Van Gogh enables us to look at the world with new eyes; to see things as we have never seen them before. To observe with him for a few minutes the beauty contained in *Starry Night* is to be invited to celebrate the deep vitality of life. Art is the echo of the divine within our being. At its best it calls to us and summons us to remember who we are. Some have seen creativity as a divine wellspring bubbling up within people, and certainly Christians should be able to recognize the hint of God within creative expression.

Cultural engagement

While the raw material of art may be found in the vaults of the imagination, the medium in which it is presented is that of culture. An artist who is ignorant of cultural context will be a poor artist. There is an element of dialogue within art; an ongoing conversation of the artist with the symbols and beliefs of contemporary society. In this way the work of a preacher has some similarities with that of the artist—both attempt to translate a vision in such a way that it will engage with their surrounding worlds. For both, an awareness of the issues in the culture is essential, as well as a commitment to participation. In this important way, artists serve as cultural analysts, albeit on the representational rather than the analytical level.

Since the collapse of Christendom, with its universal and sympathetic world-view, and the new pluralism occasioned by the Reformation in the sixteenth century, Christians have been struggling to know how to relate to culture. The fall from the position of being in authority and therefore a culture-maker and -bearer has never quite been recovered from. The first flush of liberal response was for theology to become an enthusiastic partner of the new scientific age, with the demythologizing of the Christian tradition. Later, in the face of historical reminders of sin and evil in the form of world war, theology retreated to a much more defensive position in relation to culture. Karl Barth attempted to strip revelation entirely of any cultural attachment by emphasizing the 'otherness' of the in-breaking Word. In consequence, Christians have tended to huddle together and create their own sub-culture. Neither response is particularly helpful.

What is needed at this juncture in history is a radical reinterpretation both of the tradition (including scripture) and of the culture. Both must be experienced at depth, and not in isolation from each other. The first requirement of prophets has always been that they be of the people, in the sense that they strongly identified with the group and the culture they were speaking into. Their first task, therefore, was a deep listening to both God and context, in order that their words might be doubly authentic. It may well be that in our era, artists become the prophets and bearers of God's word. Certainly they are of supreme importance when it comes to translating the Bible into a very different era.

In one sense all art is mission. In another, whenever art becomes mission, it fails to be art. Evangelistic zeal has done great harm to Christian art by insisting that it be a message bearer. Artists who are also Christians have come under great pressure to ensure that their work 'communicates' the faith. Good artists know that whenever a work of art becomes a vehicle for something other than itself, it ceases to be art. I once attended an evening when a woman was speaking on what it means to be a Christian artist. She was young, and brought along her very conservative pastor to help her out. He launched into a long diatribe about the temptation for artists to glorify themselves instead of God. One got the impression that art was a very grubby activity indeed, and only sanctified by overt Christian content. The funny thing was that the art which the woman produced was highly stylized furniture. I had difficulty in detecting what was particularly Christian about a chair!

If artists are to engage with scripture, it will not be for the purpose of promoting or proclaiming the Bible. It will rather be a confrontation between an artist who is immersed in the emerging culture and the abiding stories of scripture. Out of that confrontation creative works may spring in many forms. There can be no expectations placed on the outcome. Certainly it is not likely, even if possible, that the resultant work of art will in itself lead anyone to faith. Whether or not such an event is imaginable should not be of any concern whatsoever to the artist. The task is to bring the whole of the person to the whole of scripture, and be faithful to whatever expression results. In an oblique way, however, such art funds the cultural imagination in a way that makes reflection on religious matters feasible for the general population. That is a vital role in the current state of affairs, and a valid contribution to the mission of the church.

Can art be Christian?

Christianity and art both drive to the very heart of being. The symbols, language and rituals of faith are deeply formative of those who participate in them. But expressing art is not a matter of simply 'applying' faith to the creative endeavour. Rather, the artist reaches into the murky depths of the psyche where primal good and evil still struggle, and dredges up material to the surface. It may not be pretty; it may not look very 'Christian'. The only thing that in fact distinguishes such art as Christian is the allegiance of the artist. A Christian lawyer will not be expected somehow to establish forgiveness as the guiding principle of the legal system. Neither should we require or even encourage Christian artists to be responsible for producing an artistic interpretation of the gospel. Art doesn't need to be artificially spiritualized; it is, if genuine, already a spiritual act.

Art and the Bible

Undoubtedly, the majority of Western art has been influenced by Christianity in some way. The bulk of such art was produced at a time when the church occupied a position of high cultural authority. Whether it be a loss or a blessing, those times have gone and are unlikely to return. An artist encountering scripture in the current cultural climate is dealing not with central and universally held symbols of orthodoxy, but with a marginalized text which yet is a bearer of cultural memory. In that setting, the possibility exists of a freshness and freedom of encounter, and for a potent creative outcome. These are high times for artists to delve into the rich resources of the Bible, and allow their imaginations to be touched by the immensity of the vista.

It is a foolhardy person who makes suggestions to artists. The following examples are given by way of illustration only, and intended only to demonstrate the scope of possibility.

Painting

One of New Zealand's greatest painters was Colin McCahon. He was a rather disreputable Catholic, with a love for and unique vision of the land of New Zealand. Some of his most striking works are huge canvases with words of scripture scrawled roughly across them. In one, he depicted the simple phrase 'I AM' from Exodus 3:14 in massive letters. The scale of it is such that it causes weakness in the knees when first encountered. Another painting, entitled *The valley of dry bones*, pictures Ezekiel against the backdrop of New Zealand hills, with a cartoon bubble in which he pleads, 'Come from the four winds, O Breath, and breathe upon these slain, that they may live' (Ezekiel 37:9). Yet another, *A grain of wheat*, consists of white script on a black background, bearing the words of John 12:24, 'In truth, in very truth I tell you, a grain of wheat remains a solitary grain; unless it falls into the ground and dies, but if it dies it becomes a rich harvest.'

In much of his work there is a fascination with the text of scripture, and particularly with strangely resonant phrases. His presentation of such texts creates a sense of encounter which is unavoidable. There is some irony in the fact that many of those who admire McCahon, and find the words in his work compelling, have little idea of their source. His interpretation is not limited to the raw text of the Bible. He depicts biblical events such as the Annunciation in the context of local geography, in so doing closing the distance between scripture and contemporary life. His work contains genius, and has of recent times come to international attention. McCahon represents one possibility of a painter encountering the Bible.

Sculpture

Another New Zealand artist who was also a Catholic was Ria Bancroft. Her sculptures address a variety of themes, many of them reflections on biblical events such as the crucifixion or Mary holding the body of the crucified Jesus. Although she was an active Christian, she disliked the label 'religious' being applied to her work, considering it a simplistic and reductionist description to use of art. Bancroft's sculpting can be stark or luxurious. A crucifix she fashioned is dark and haunting. The bronze statue is set on a base of greywhacke, New Zealand's ubiquitous river stone. Like McCahon, she chooses to bring the biblical world into her own immediate environment. Her description of the creative process was enlightening: 'I am merely the vehicle, the person who brings the work into being without really knowing why.'

For the doors of the tabernacle in the Cathedral of the Blessed Sacrament in Christchurch, Bancroft fashioned a bronze relief which shows Jesus being taken down from the cross on one panel, and rising again to new life on the other. It is a spectacular and tender depiction, which so caught the imagination of Bishop John V. Taylor that he used a photo of it for the cover of one of his books. Another of her works, entitled *The Kingdom*, consists of a brass cross mounted atop a large sphere of dark volcanic rock, and bearing the injunction 'Thy kingdom come'. To reach out and touch these sculptures and feel their message provides an entirely different way of encountering scripture from that of reading.

I was impressed during a visit to the Church of the Saviour, a non-denominational community in America's capital city, by a sculpture which had been commissioned by the congregation, and mounted outside on the footpath. The community in which the church exists is one of the poorest and most violent in the city. And there, out on the street, sits Jesus. While I watched, a Central American immigrant carried his small child to the statue so that she could kiss Jesus. Others told me that they had seen drunks sit on the knee of Jesus and offer him a drink from their bottle. Out there in the noise and chaos of the street, this representation of the Son of God proclaims the divine presence and companionship in a more tangible form than preaching, and has become a loved addition to community life.

Film

Film is both an immensely popular form of art, and the central vehicle for discussion of issues within the emerging culture. Increasingly, the broad issue of spirituality is gaining attention in the world of cinema. To date, films which have been produced from an overtly 'Christian' base, bearing some sort of not too subtle message, have ranged from the simple to the dreadfully simplistic. On the other hand, there have been some superb treatments crafted by people who don't necessarily classify themselves as Christian at all. The best treatment of the life of Jesus, for example, has to be Denys Arcand's stunning *Jesus of Montreal*. Not only did it bring to life some of the less accessible nuances of the Gospels, it was also a wonderfully crafted movie, winning the jury prize at the Cannes Festival. Some of the reinterpretations of the biblical material such as the cleansing of the temple and the temptation of Jesus are riveting.

Other films take a more oblique approach to biblical themes. *Priest* highlights the tension between the institutional church and the gospel of forgiveness, as it traverses the perilous territory of homosexuality and forbidden love in the lives of priests and parishioners. *Dead Man Walking* explores the complex interrelationship between sin and the hunger for reconciliation, in the story of a man sentenced to death by lethal injection. The final scene of execution with its cruciform analogy serves to evoke religious undertones, and present hope against the gritty background of rape and murder. *Secrets and Lies* is an extended commentary on the destructive power of guilt, and the need for confession, in the context of a young woman unexpectedly tracing her birth mother. Good films allow enough space and freedom for the viewer to find their own place among the characters and issues. While there may be confrontation with religious themes, it is not in a proselytizing sense.

Music

The church has a rich tradition in the field of music. Many of the finest musical accomplishments of Western culture have their locus in Christian worship. Anyone who listens to the classics finds themselves immersed in theological symbols and themes. From the majesty of Bach's *Jesu, Joy of Man's Desiring* to the sheer transcendence of Handel's *Messiah*, the mysteries of faith have been rendered in glorious harmony. Today still, despite the declining numbers and influence of the church in the West, the Christian community continues as a bastion of fine music. Classical composers in particular find in the church not only venues with appropriate ambience, but a sympathetic cultural community where the traditions of fine music are still appreciated. Unfortunately some of those who acclaim such church music are as little affected by the words or themes contained therein as they are by the Italian of opera.

In the field of contemporary Christian music, there has been an explosive growth in the number of bands. Many of these are aware of the importance which music has in youth culture, as an arena where issues of meaning are aired and debated. Well-intentioned Christian groups and performers seek to inject their faith into the discussion. Unfortunately, 'message' often dominates, and there is not enough concern with musical credibility. A more balanced approach would be that of Canadian singer/songwriter Bruce Cockburn, who says:

> *My faith determines how I see things, so the way I write my songs will be affected by that very much. But I don't see the music as a means of selling the faith. It doesn't feel right to me. Songs are an expression of things I feel and see, things that touch me. Therefore, my faith comes into it indirectly, determining my reaction to what I see and experience.* [13]

If there is to be a meaningful engagement of contemporary music with the Bible, it will come from the sort of dedication and approach of people like Cockburn.

Writing

I suppose my favourite writer addressing Christian themes is Graham Greene. At a young age, I was deeply influenced by *The Power and the Glory*. Its contrast between a sin-tarnished whiskey priest and the pristine ideological orthodoxy of the captain of police reveals nothing so strongly as the abiding grace of God. Greene has an intimate knowledge of the frailty and corruption of human nature, and its insignificance in the light of divine love. He knows himself, and he knows God. It is not necessary for Greene to set out to prove anything. He simply tells a story, and through that story the mercy of God bleeds. I think all potential Pharisees would be well served by reading either *The Power and the Glory* or *Monsignor Quixote*. They will gain a greater understanding of the scandal of Jesus' forgiveness of sinners.

There are other writers who have been able to bring spiritual reality to credible life through their work. Among them I would count T.S. Eliot, C.S. Lewis, Flannery O'Connor, Frederick Buechner, Susan Howatch and Tim Winton. All these are marked by their understanding of the ambiguity and pain of human existence, and yet manage to suffuse their works with love and hope. In this way they are making a gospel declaration even if they never mention the gospel. In their writings, the word becomes Word, bringing God closer to the reader. Scripture is a rich resource for all writers, and aspiring authors could do worse than to immerse themselves in the rhythms and riches of the Bible.

Dance

We are embodied creatures, much to the disdain of those who have promoted an ultimately heretical form of falsely ascetic Christianity. The Bible acknowledges the legitimacy and appropriateness of dance as a form of response to God. A word of warning is necessary here. I am not a fan of what a friend of mine calls 'ribbon-wavers'. Such people feel that their gift to the congregation is to leap up during songs and make embarrassing and frequently suggestive movements at the front of the church. In so doing, they draw attention to themselves, and frequently put the other worshippers off their lunch. Good performance dance can be powerfully engaging on its own; unfortunately I haven't seen much of it within the walls of churches.

Much more interesting is the corporate involvement in dance, where movement of the body by ordinary worshippers becomes a form of response to God. Although this may seem like purgatory to some Christian people, the popularity of clubbing and dance music would indicate that the culture is receptive to it. I have experienced various forms of congregational dance; from the legendary 'charismatic two-step' (a foot-shuffle accommodated to the limited space of worship auditoriums), to folk dancing with everyone up and in a circle, to raging to dance music in an alternative worship setting. It is this last form which I suspect holds the most promise. There is something about dancing to good music while giant images on the wall bear the words of scripture, which helps to integrate text and body and soul at a deep level. I imagine there is scope for good dance artists and choreographers to present and interpret scripture, and this awaits development.

Installation art

A few years back I was in Canberra, Australia, for a conference. I had spare time, and so wandered through the National Art Gallery, which was superb. Downstairs there was a special exhibition of installation art. One of the works moved me to tears. To get to it, it was necessary to walk down a tunnel. Along the walls were words spelling out an incident in the Rwandan massacre, in which a young girl watched as her family was killed before her eyes. Emerging into a large room, I found a huge table piled high with 35mm slides. Attached by wires to the side of the table were hand-held slide viewers. I popped a slide into the viewer, and found the eyes of a Rwandan girl staring out at me. I chose another. They were all the same. There were thousands and thousands of them; as many as had been killed in the massacres. It was a complex interaction—me looking on as an indifferent bystander, and these thousands of pairs of eyes looking out at me pleading.

This sort of art offers real possibility for creative interaction with scripture. Mark Pierson, minister of Cityside Baptist Church in Auckland and instigator of Parallel Universe (an alternative worship community), has twice organized Easter art installations. This involved providing space and co-ordinating the work of local artists, who were invited to choose one of the traditional stations of the cross and reflect upon it in any medium of their choosing. The results have been outstanding, ranging from elaborate video loops running on cruciform TV screens to a face-wiping exercise in which the cloth used became transformed with the image of Jesus' face. One intriguing video loop contained words of scripture from Luke 23:28 and 29 scrolling slowly down the screen over appropriate background images. The annual event is much more than an art show; it is an act of meditative worship, facilitated by artists.

Banners

In my days at Ponsonby Baptist Church, we were lucky to have in the congregation someone who took the making of banners seriously. Beryl Turner had recently graduated from theological college, and in the absence of a call to full-time ministry was helping out at Ponsonby. She undertook the making of a set of banners to mark the church year. The building with a 30ft-high ceiling lent itself to dramatic lengths of cloth. Beryl would spend weeks preparing the design of each banner; thinking about the particular season, reading the Bible, and dreaming of how she might interpret it. Frequently she consulted with other members of the congregation. It is not much help trying to describe the beautiful and inspiring icons which she produced. But even in the dullest of services, people were able to look at those banners and be lifted toward God.

In Parallel Universe, artistic members of the community were given great lengths of sheeting fabric and asked to paint them. Without any guidance, they produced vivid and striking banners which became part of the visual experience of worship every time we met. One of them was a reflection on Luke 19:40, 'I tell you, if these were silent, the stones would shout out.' And then there was our theme banner, which encapsulated the ethos of Parallel Universe:

> *Are you tired? Worn out? Burned out on religion? Come to me. Get away with me and you'll recover your life. I'll show you how to take a real rest. Walk with me and work with me—watch how I do it. Learn the unforced rhythms of grace. I won't lay anything heavy or ill-fitting on you. Keep company with me and you'll learn to live freely and lightly.* (Matthew 11:28–30, *The Message*)

There are other art forms, and as many ways of bringing them into dialogue with the Bible as there are creative minds. Allowing art to be a form of responding to scripture is a way of breaking it free from rationalist shackles. One of the most important functions of the church in coming years may well be to nourish, protect and encourage artists. They bear in their hearts and imaginations the soul of the gospel, and we are sorely in need of it.

[CONCLUSION]

It Cuts Both Ways

As the Gospel of John states so succinctly, 'In the beginning was the Word, and the Word was with God, and the Word was God' (John 1:1). We have already seen that there is no simple equation between the Word and the Bible. But without the Bible, we have limited access to the Word. A home page is not the person who lies behind it. And yet, it is a form of self-communication by its compiler, reflecting something of who they are. The Bible is a very important element in God's self-communication with humanity. It leads us to the feet of Jesus, and Jesus is the Word of God. To return to John, 'And the Word became flesh and lived among us, and we have seen his glory, the glory as of a father's only son, full of grace and truth' (John 1:14).

There is a sense of tragedy in the current tendency to either neglect or trivialize the Bible. At the very time when the modernist paradigm with all its aridity is falling away, it seems that Christians are experiencing the contempt of familiarity in regard to the scriptures. Perhaps it will take a fresh wave of immigrants to the faith to rekindle passion for the Bible. When we lose our hold on the Bible, we lose our memory of what it means to be followers of Jesus Christ. Without the constant subversive voice of scripture, institutional forces within the church are enabled to dominate. If the people of God lose touch with their history and place of standing, they are cut off from their source of life and perspective. Once the foundations go, there is little hope for the superstructure.

As a means of gaining some final overview of the role of scripture, if may be worth examining a few selected images from within the Bible which speak of the power and purpose of the Word of God. Once again, we need to make the qualification that the book lying on the desk with two covers and ink on pages is not yet the Word of God. But for those who open it with a prayer in their heart, it may well become that.

A two-edged sword

There are few better analogies for the role the Bible is capable of playing than these words from Hebrews:

> *Indeed, the word of God is living and active, sharper than any two-edged sword, piercing until it divides soul from spirit, joints from marrow; it is able to judge the thoughts and intentions of the heart. (Hebrews 4:12)*

My knowledge of swords is rather limited. I presume the advantage of a two-edged sword is that it cuts both ways. In a different era, the comparison might have been made with a scalpel. It is sharp, it is dangerous and it is penetrating. You don't fool around with either two-edged swords or scalpels unless you are serious. Otherwise you end up unnecessarily hurt.

All of us are involved in game-playing. We hide from the truth, we hide from ourselves, we hide from others and we hide from God. Our lives are full of brokenness, hypocrisy and betrayal, and there are few among us who are willing to live in full knowledge of their own character. Self-deception may be the most dangerous of all forms of deception, but that doesn't stop us from practising it. Most of us have become adept at fashioning images of ourselves which are more acceptable than the reality, and then presenting this image to the world. We easily find people who will reinforce our illusions, provided we return the favour and support theirs. It is dangerously easy to lose touch with the truth.

Scott Peck has written about what he calls 'people of the lie'. In his book of that title, he describes the way in which self-deception can get out of hand within human life, and allow for the entry of evil. Of people who have succumbed, he writes:

The words 'image', 'appearance', and 'outwardly' are crucial to understanding the morality of the evil. While they seem to lack any motivation to be good, they intensely desire to appear good. Their 'goodness' is all on a level of pretense. It is, in effect, a lie. This why they are the 'people of the lie', Actually, the lie is designed not so much to deceive others as to deceive themselves.[14]

While this represents an extreme condition within human experience, it also speaks to us of the dangers of persisting in self-deception.

It is possible for not just individuals, but entire societies fundamentally to lose touch with the basics of human existence, and the categories of right and wrong. The classic example of this within the twentieth century was Germany under the rule of Hitler. But an equal case might be made for the current ideological delusion which has infected the West under the name of economic rationalism. The focus on the wealthy and the strong, the attack on concepts of common responsibility, the neglect of those within the community least able to defend themselves; all these are indicators of a society which has constructed a lie for itself, and then climbed inside and inhabited it.

In order to evaluate such delusions, there needs to be a source of perspective. It is essential to have a means of cutting away that which is false and self-justifying. There must be a means of penetrating the ambiguity engendered by propaganda. In this respect, the Bible has no peer. Scripture is razor-sharp and dangerous; as Hebrews has it, 'able to judge the thoughts and intentions of the heart'. Whether deception arises in the lives of individuals or of communities, the Bible is able to slice it away and lay bare the truth. It bears a reminder of what the nature and purpose of humanity is, and contains the wisdom of a thousand generations who have sought to distort reality to their own ends. In the murk of falsehood, the Word of God sounds clear and true.

A seed

In the well-known parable of the sower, Jesus identifies the seed as 'the word' (Mark 4:14). The seed lodges within the hearts of its hearers and, where it finds fertile soil, springs up to produce a bountiful crop. This image speaks to us of the potential of scripture. A seed is very deceptive. It is tiny, dry and unattractive. There is little hint given by its appearance of what it may become. But give it the right conditions, and a miracle takes place. The seed contains within itself the possibility of life. From small and humble beginnings, it bursts out into growth and fruitfulness, eventually producing a full-grown plant out of all proportion to its initial state. There have been seeds found in the tombs of Egyptian pharaohs which, when planted after thousands of years of dormancy, have germinated and grown to maturity.

These are difficult times in which we live. In an age of cynicism and mistrust, very often the seed of the Bible falls on hard hearts. The soil is hard and dry from carrying too much traffic. As New Zealand poet James K. Baxter has said, making known the gospel in today's society is like planting cabbages in concrete. People are not so much resistant to the notion that God loves them, as indifferent. But we should not lose confidence in the seed in times when conditions for its growth are adverse. Like those tiny bearers of life locked up in the vaults of Egypt, the resilient power of the word to spring into growth should not be underestimated. All the potential of life is locked up within it, simply waiting for nourishment.

Like a seed, the Bible requires little to get it started. A small place in the soul, a little light and water, and the process begins. Sometimes it is not until the harrows of suffering break up the topsoil that such a place is found. The germinated seed grows in two directions: sinking roots down into the substratum of our hearts, and sending up tendrils into the open arena of our minds and actions. While young, it is still at risk. It may be plucked up, or shrivel from neglect or sarcasm. But given time and space, scripture will become abundant and luxuriant, greening the soul and producing fruit beyond our imagination. It is a mystery, this process of growth. We don't control it or direct it. Our responsibility is simply that of providing a place for it to develop.

A mirror

This time in history probably contains more mirrors than in the rest of human civilization put together, and less genuine self-reflection than any other. The mirrors we use are those which are limited to the surface of our lives only. That is where the focus of the culture seems to lie, and inordinate attention is given to the outer dimension of existence. To use Jesus' analogy of an earlier era with some similarities to our own, it is as if we were obsessed with the elaborate façade of a tomb, while ignorant of the fact that inside it there are putrefying corpses (Matthew 23:27–28). Our society is narcissistic in the extreme, captivated by its own reflection but spending little time pondering the deeper questions of existence or meaning.

What is needed is a mirror of the soul; a mirror which will reflect for us the inner conditions of our hearts. It is in just those terms that James describes the word of God:

> But be doers of the word, and not merely hearers who deceive
> themselves. For if any are hearers of the word and not doers,
> they are like those who look at themselves in a mirror; for they
> look at themselves and, on going away, immediately forget
> what they were like. (James 1:22–24)

The Bible gives an accurate image of the inner complexion of our hearts; a vision which can be unwelcome. It is possible for those who are the most beautiful in their outward appearance to be full of ugly motives and intentions. I have known people with a great fear of the Bible, because of the way in which it has exposed the less attractive interior of their hearts.

If scripture has become less prominent in the life of worshipping communities, we may suspect that the neglect is partially due to that which congregations see when they look into it. They may prefer some other form of reflective surface in which the image returned is not nearly so sharp or intimate. But it is those who are sick who desperately need to understand what is happening on the inside of them. The purpose of a doctor's examination is not to harm but to heal. In the same way, the mirror of the Bible is intended to expose the ludicrous nature of our self-justification, and lead us into the arms of God. There will be an inevitable time for each of us when cosmetics fail to conceal our true natures, and it is best to come to terms with this in the course of life rather than after it.

A lamp

I remember a time walking home from the village of Kuranda in the north of Queensland. I lived at the time in a commune amidst the rainforest, some miles out of town. It was late at night, and there was only just enough light to distinguish the road from the surrounding vegetation. While strolling along, I stepped into the midst of what appeared to be a coil of rope discarded on the road. A few paces further on, an awful thought struck me. I carefully retraced my steps, and discovered what I'd feared was true. In all innocence, I had all but trodden on a snake which lay coiled before me. For the remainder of the journey home, I strained my eyes into the darkness to check where I was walking.

There are times when we are in desperate need of a little light to show us where we are walking. In Psalm 119, scripture is regarded as just such a source of light: 'Your word is a lamp to my feet and a light to my path' (Psalm 119:105). When the age is dark, any extra light on our paths is a great help. For many of us, our lives are full of complex choices. We face moral issues in unexplored territory, and there is little to help us find a way forward. Geneticists, managers, lawyers and parents are but some of the groups confounded by an era where the choices keep spiralling out of control, and the guidance needed to make them is distinctly lacking. The Bible will not, despite the claims of some, provide clear-cut answers as to which paths we should choose. However, in our journey into uncertainty, it will provide a reliable source of light to shine on the way.

Another time I was travelling late at night with my family in the car. The others had fallen asleep. It was deep in the countryside on a gravel road, where there were no street lights. I rounded a corner, and was confronted by a narrow one-way bridge. As the car sped towards it, I reached down to turn on the heater. Inadvertently, I hit the wrong switch and turned off the headlights. Immediately everything was pitch black. There was no time to do anything, but to try to remember the image of the bridge, and hold my course. We survived, but only because I'd had a good look at what lay ahead while the lights were on. The Bible serves to light up our way, so that we at least have some understanding of what we are confronting. If we remain faithful to what we see in its light, it gives us hope in our navigation of the road ahead.

Fire

The prophet Jeremiah compares the word of the Lord to fire (Jeremiah 23:29). Fire serves a number of purposes. It provides warmth, it consumes and it purifies. All of these attributes are shared by the Bible. In the cold winds of isolation and despair, scripture serves as a welcoming beacon, with its reminder that every member of humanity has a place of belonging in the divine heart. These are times of alienation and disconnection, when many people experience loneliness and rejection. Scripture reminds us constantly that we are loved for nothing other than our being. The messages abroad in the world do their best to convince us that we can only be valued and accepted through our possessions or achievements. Only a regular reminder God's love is unconditional will suffice to drown out these discouraging voices. The assurance of acceptance is such that it warms us from the inside.

But the fire is also dangerous. It consumes that which is combustible. In 1 Corinthians, Paul reminds us that the quality of our faith may be sifted, 'because it will be revealed with fire, and the fire will test what sort of work has been done' (1 Corinthians 3:13). This quality of fire is the essence of its use in purification. Although the prospect of fire is daunting, it is 'so that the genuineness of your faith—being more precious than gold that, though perishable, is tested by fire—may be found to result in praise and glory and honour when Jesus Christ is revealed' (1 Peter 1:7). The encounter with scripture on a regular basis serves to strip away that which demeans our human nature, and to temper the qualities necessary for the life of faith. The Bible is the furnace of God through which we must pass, but we need have no fear in the midst of it.

Life-giver

In one of the loveliest passages of Hebrew poetry in the Bible, God speaks words of comfort through the prophet Isaiah:

> For as the rain and the snow come down from heaven,
>   and do not return there until they have watered the earth,
> making it bring forth and sprout,
>   giving seed to the sower and bread to the eater,
> so shall my word be that goes out from my mouth;
>   it shall not return to me empty,
> but it will accomplish that which I purpose,
>   and succeed in the thing for which I sent it. (Isaiah 55:10, 11)

This is a beautiful assurance of the life-giving and nurturing qualities of God's word. It is as abundant and as freely available as the rain; as staple and sustaining as bread. The word of God proceeds from God, and because of that has the ability to bring life and growth to all that it touches.

My experience of the rainy season in tropical climates has given me new appreciation of the rain. Previously I had thought of rain as something cold and depressing, an affliction to be sheltered from. But in warmer regions, the rain is heavy, impenetrable and tepid. In my first experiences of it, I stripped down to my shorts, threw back my head and laughed and danced in it. In many lands, the onset of the rain is the guarantee of continued fertility and harvest, and therefore a cause for celebration. In a similar way, the Bible brings with it the certainty of new growth. It brings the life of nutrients to starved roots, and washes away accumulated dust from tired leaves so that they can breathe again. There is a trail of greenery which follows in its path.

On my first encounter with scripture in that hotel room in Sydney, I had no idea of the role it was to play in my life. I could not have imagined the growth it would unleash within my jaded spirit, nor the sustenance it would provide over the long haul. Over the years there has been flourishing foliage and severe pruning. The one constant has been that the Bible has been a source of life to me; life of the sort which is not easily extinguished. This is not my experience alone, but that of millions of people in hugely different times and contexts. God has spoken and speaks. The Bible gives us access both to that which has been spoken, and, even more importantly, to the speaker. That which goes out from the mouth of God accomplishes that for which it has been sent.

I began this journey around the mountain of scripture with the hope and prayer that the sky might clear somewhat in the travelling, in order to reveal the ancient peak in all its glory. Along the way, I have discovered again how massive and daunting the Bible is. We may talk all we wish; it abides. If scaling the heights should have fallen out of fashion for a time, it will not harm the mountain. It waits there for us, beckoning with majesty and challenge. People may throw stones, or shield their eyes from this presence which looms on the horizon. The mountain simply stands and waits. And beyond it, God.

References

1   Oliver Sacks, *The Man Who Mistook his Wife for a Hat*, Picador, 1985.

2   Mike Riddell, *Godzone: A Guide to the Travels of the Soul*, Lion, 1992.

3   Martin Wroe, *When You Haven't Got a Prayer*, Lion, 1997.

4   St Augustine, *Confessions*, Book I, Section 1. Various contemporary translations of this Christian classic are available.

5   Mike Riddell, *alt.spirit@metro.m3: An Alternative Spirituality for the Third Millennium*, Lion, 1997, p.10.

6   John V. Taylor, *The Go-Between God: The Holy Spirit and the Christian Mission*, SCM, 1972, p.16f.

7   Frederick Buechner, *Wishful Thinking: A Seeker's ABC*, HarperSanFrancisco, 1993, p.120.

8   Frederick Buechner, *Telling Secrets*, HarperSanFrancisco, 1991, p.36.

9   Frederick Buechner, *Telling Secrets*, p.36.

10   Kurt Cobain, *Smells Like Teen Spirit*, 1991, DGC

11   Walter Wink, *Transforming Bible Study*, SCM, 1981.

12   M. Scott Peck, *The Different Drum*, Simon Schuster, 1988, p.56f.

13   Quoted in Steve Turner, *Hungry for Heaven: Rock and Roll and the Search for Redemption*, Virgin, 1988, p.166.

14   M. Scott Peck, *People of the Lie*, Simon & Schuster, 1983, p.75.